PENGUIN BOOKS

Caring for Older People

Dr J. A. Muir Gray was born and brought up in Glasgow and attended medical school there. After a brief period in hospital medicine he entered the field of public health, and worked first in the City of Oxford Public Health Department and then from 1974 for the Oxfordshire Health Authority. Dr Gray's main interests are preventive medicine and the problems of elderly people, and he has published a number of books on these subjects for those who are looking after elderly relatives at home. He has also published *Geriatric Problems in General Practice, Man Against Disease*, and is the editor of *Preventive Medicine in General Practice*. Dr Gray is the honorary secretary to ASH (Action on Smoking and Health), a member of the Health Education Council, and is a vice-president of the Health Visitors' Association. He is married with two small daughters.

Heather McKenzie, a barrister, author, and director of the National Council for Carers and their Elderly Dependants, is acknowledged as the international expert in this field. Her other books on the subject are *Take Care of Your Elderly Relative, You Alone Care* and the *Getting On Catalogue*. She writes and broadcasts extensively on caring. Heather McKenzie is married to Dr Norman Lovat, a physicist. They have a daughter.

J. A. Muir Gray MD
Heather McKenzie LLB

Caring for Older People

Penguin Books

Penguin Books Ltd, Harmondsworth, Middlesex, England
Viking Penguin Inc., 40 West 23rd Street, New York, New York 10010, U.S.A.
Penguin Books Australia Ltd, Ringwood, Victoria, Australia
Penguin Books Canada Ltd, 2801 John Street, Markham, Ontario, Canada L3R 1B4
Penguin Books (N.Z.) Ltd, 182–190 Wairau Road, Auckland 10, New Zealand

First published 1986

Made and printed in Great Britain by
Richard Clay (The Chaucer Press) Ltd, Bungay, Suffolk
Filmset in 10/13 pt Monophoto Photina

To our own families – in all generations

Contents

Preface

The family forms the main source of support for disabled elderly people. There is no evidence that the modern family cares less well for its disabled elders than did the families of yesteryear. Too often, however, the family itself is not given sufficient support, and in this book we describe some of the ways in which the demands of caring can be made less stressful.

Each family is unique and finds its own ways of coping. What we have recorded are some of the ways in which other people have coped with common problems, and some of the tips and ideas that relatives and friends have found helpful and have passed on to us. There is often more than one way of looking at a problem and where appropriate – as in the cases of incontinence and mental confusion – we have included more than one perspective.

We have used the terms 'he' and 'she', 'elder' and 'parent' in different parts of the text wherever it seemed most appropriate to do so. These are simply a shorthand way of writing 'the elderly person you are caring for' and do not signify that the advice relates only to a 'he' or a 'she' or a 'parent' or an 'elder'.

We hope that you will find this book helps you to cope with the challenge of caring well for an old person. Please let us have any advice you would wish to pass on to other people in your position.

Muir Gray   Heather McKenzie

CHAPTER 1

Understanding Old Age

Shakespeare wrote of the Seven Ages of Man: nowadays most people think of three – childhood, adult life and old age, with retirement the gateway between adult life and old age. Biologically, however, there are only two phases in life – the phase of growth and development, and the phase of decline during which the ageing processes are dominant.

There are many different ageing processes. Their net effect is to reduce the body's ability to respond quickly and appropriately to challenges such as infection or dehydration, or a change in environmental temperature. The young person in a cold room will react quickly so that his body conserves heat and maintains a constant body temperature; an aged person in the same environment will react more slowly and less completely. Indeed, his reaction may be so inadequate that his body temperature will fall and fall until he develops hypothermia.

Many people assume that the ageing process is also responsible for the progressive decline in physical ability which affects almost everyone as they grow older. For most people this decline starts in their early twenties. The reason it usually starts about then is not that the ageing processes become dominant when adolescence is over, but that most people start to lose fitness in their early twenties.

Fitness and Ageing

Normal employment and housework make few physical demands on the majority of people. They therefore start to lose their fitness from the moment they stop playing physical sports – for many people this means as soon as they leave school or college. All of the four main aspects of fitness are lost – strength, stamina, suppleness and skill. The rate at which an individual declines is therefore determined by the rate at which he loses fitness as well as by the rate of the ageing process. The gap between how much you are able to do and how much you could do if you were fully fit – the fitness gap – widens with age, but it can be closed at any age. Strength, stamina, suppleness and skill can be improved at any age.

Disease and Ageing

Many diseases occur more commonly in old age, but this does not mean that all such diseases are caused by ageing. Some diseases do indeed appear to be closely related to the normal process of ageing – cataract, for example – but the majority of serious diseases do not appear to be the result of the ageing process. The increased rate of disease in old age often simply reflects the fact that old people have lived longer than young people! Take cancer, for example. Most cancers are more common in old age, and at one time it was thought that all ageing resulted in cancer. It is now known, however, that almost all cancers are caused by environmental factors, and for this reason the disease is more common among old people than young people. It is not surprising that people who have smoked cigarettes for fifty years are more likely to develop cancer than those who have only smoked for ten years.

Ageing Or Disease?

Ageing and disease can both cause problems such as breathlessness, weakness or forgetfulness, so how can an old person decide whether to consult his doctor, or to accept the problem as being just 'old age'?

The best guide is given by the time it has taken for the problem to develop. If it has developed slowly over a number of years, almost imperceptibly, it is probably due to ageing, often combined with loss of fitness. If, on the other hand, it has developed over a few days or a few weeks, it is probably due to a disease. For example:

Mr S has noticed that he is now more breathless after climbing the stairs to his flat than he was when he moved in twenty-four years ago.

Mr T notices that he is more breathless when climbing the stairs to his daughter's flat than he was when he visited her five days previously.

Mr S is probably affected by ageing and loss of fitness; Mr T probably has a disease, and should consult his general practitioner.

The rule is that if you, or your relative, can identify the problem as having a recent, relatively sudden onset – 'it started at Whitsun', or 'it's just been the last three weeks' – disease should be suspected and a doctor consulted. If, on the other hand, the problem has been coming on for years it is less likely to be due to disease. It will more likely, but not inevitably, be due to the effects of ageing and the loss of fitness.

Ageing, Disease and Loss of Fitness

When disease strikes, the rate of decline often increases. This is not only because of the effects of ageing and the disease processes, but also because an old person with a disease usually loses fitness more quickly than someone of the same age who does not have that disease. Sometimes the disease itself results in inactivity; sometimes it is the belief of the old person and his family that a disabled person should always 'take it easy'. Whatever the reason, the effect is the same – a drop in activity and fitness.

Activity may be unwise in the acute phase of an illness, but the majority of people with a chronic disease should try to keep active to ensure that the fitness gap does not become even wider.

It is also important to remember that disease in old age does not always produce symptoms such as pain or breathlessness. Sometimes the only early sign of disease is a decrease in the person's ability to do something. For example:

Mr B has always enjoyed eighteen holes of golf, but for the last three weeks he has only been able to manage nine holes because his muscles feel too tired to continue.

Miss C is eighty and has always gone upstairs to bed. One evening she finds she is too breathless to reach the top of the stairs and has to go back down and sleep in a chair.

If an old person suddenly becomes unable to perform a task that he was previously able to do, it is possible that disease and not normal ageing is the cause. Medical advice should therefore be sought.

Disease, Disability, Handicap and Dependence

Diseases have different effects. Some of them – diabetes, for example – have few noticeable effects on the individual's daily life, although they do increase that person's risk of early death. Many diseases, however, restrict the sufferer's ability to look after himself or his ability to get about outside his house. Those which impair self-care and mobility are called the disabling diseases. A disability may be defined as a loss of function, such as losing the ability to climb stairs. A disability may be caused by any one of a number of diseases – immobility may be caused by Parkinson's disease or arthritis or a stroke.

One handicap is the social problem that results from a disability. A person who is unable to go out because of his immobility is no longer able to reach the church or go to the shops, and he may also be financially poorer because he can no longer shop around for the best buys.

Dependence is an important type of handicap – the reliance on other people for tasks that most people take for granted. No one, of course, is completely independent. We all depend on other people, but most people are able to perform the following tasks without assistance:

- dressing and undressing
- washing all over
- getting enough to eat and drink
- reaching the toilet in time
- doing the housework and gardening
- getting into and out of bed.

Many disabled people have to rely on other people for such tasks, either partially or totally. Most people find the experience depressing and some find dependence humiliating.

Some, it must be said, enjoy the company that dependence

brings, and this can affect the motivation to overcome a disability. The housebound person who is receiving home help and district nursing, in addition to help from her relatives, and who is told that she could become more independent with a new form of treatment, will probably welcome this information. But in the back of her mind may lurk the fear that any improvement the new treatment may bring will not restore full fitness to her – so that she is able, for instance, to walk to church – but will simply lead to the withdrawal of the visits of the home help and district nurse, on whom she has come to depend for personal contact and friendship, as well as for the tasks they perform.

The motives of the people on whom the older person depends are also likely to be mixed in many cases. Some people find the dependence of an old person irksome, but others enjoy the feeling of being useful, and some are glad to be able to repay the care given them by the old person when she was young and fit.

Mental Ageing

There are four processes, then, affecting the person who is growing older.

1. Ageing – a natural, biological process.
2. Loss of fitness – due to inactivity.
3. Disease – an abnormal or pathological process.
4. Social changes – such as the decline in income that occurs in old age.

These affect both mind and body, for the mind also changes as we grow older. The normal ageing of the brain results in certain changes, notably a decline in the ability to calculate as quickly, or to remember lists and names as easily, as one could when younger. These changes are also aggravated by loss of mental fitness – many people do not use their minds as much as they did when they were at school or college. The social changes which take place as we grow older can also affect intellectual function. For example, young people often fail to correct mistakes made by an older person, and will let erroneous statements pass without a word, whereas they would have challenged them if they had been made by a younger person. Disease, notably dementia (see p. 79), is also a cause of decline in cerebral ability, but it is only when disease takes a hold that a serious decline occurs.

If you reach the age of eighty, having kept yourself reasonably fit and mentally active, and have been lucky enough not to develop a disabling disease such as dementia or arthritis, you should still be able to manage the following activities:

- keep a garden, but not do heavy digging
- look after yourself
- read books and a newspaper
- enjoy a drink or two without undue effect
- enjoy a good argument
- drive a car.

So What?

The importance of these facts can be summarized simply.

1. Many problems that commonly occur in old age are preventable.
2. Few of the problems that occur in old age are caused by the ageing process: most are caused by disease, loss of fitness, or social changes, and can therefore be treated.
3. Most people are too pessimistic about the scope for improvement in old age.

CHAPTER 2

Health Maintenance and Improvement

Many people think of preventive medicine as something that is only for young people. Nothing could be further from the truth. There are many things that an old person can do to keep well and to become healthier.

Cigarette Smoking

It is sometimes said that older people should not be encouraged to stop smoking. Our view is that old people have a right to know the risks of smoking and to make up their own minds when they know them.

Pipe and cigar smoking are not particularly harmful, although cigar smokers who formerly smoked cigarettes will often inhale. The main risks are associated with cigarette smoking, in old age, as at any age. This is because it aggravates

chronic bronchitis and emphysema (see p. 60)
diseases of the arteries of the hands and lower limbs (see p. 57).

People with these diseases should be told of the risks they run and instructed how to set about stopping smoking.

Many heavy smokers find it very difficult to stop, although some people succeed even after decades of smoking. The simple rules are:

1. Give up completely: do not try to cut down gradually.
2. Take more exercise after giving up.
3. Enlist the support of friends by telling them about the attempt.
4. Keep the money saved to buy a reward.

If this does not work, a second attempt is worth while, but if that fails the advice of the general practitioner should be sought. She may recommend nicotine chewing-gum, but most people who give up do so without any type of artificial aid – they just drop the habit.

Getting Older, Getting Fitter

As we have emphasized, loss of fitness leads to loss of functional ability, but research has shown that fitness can be regained at any age. The rate of decline can be not only slowed, but even reversed – this often happens during retirement because many people find they are able to lead a healthier lifestyle than they did when they were at work.

All four aspects of physical fitness – strength, stamina, suppleness and skill – can be improved at very little risk, provided that the unfit person does not increase the amount of exercise too fast. (It makes no sense suddenly to start playing squash or running.) Even where there is chronic disease, only in rare cases will exercise not be beneficial. A person with a chronic disease, or someone who is receiving repeat prescriptions, should however first seek the advice of his doctor.

What type of exercise?

The most important type of exercise is everyday work, such as dressing and undressing, or housework and gardening. This is the occupational therapy and physiotherapy of everyday life. Too often, tasks which are keeping an old person fit are taken away from her by well-meaning neighbours and relatives, for it is a natural reaction to wish to perform a task that your elderly relative is obviously finding more difficult than she did in the past – going shopping or raking up leaves, for example. It is certainly important to ask yourself whether their difficulty is a sign of disease (see p. 69), but if it is not, it is better for old people to carry on doing what they can, particularly if they want to do so.

If your relative asks for help, even after the benefits of exercise have been explained to her, try making the task easier, for example by buying an electric lawnmower, before taking the job over completely. If she is reluctant to take your word, it may be advisable to ask the health visitor to talk to her.

Housework and gardening, though worthy pursuits, are boring to many people, and old people often prefer to take it easier at home while becoming more active outside. Suitable leisure activities for older people are walking, cycling, swimming, dancing, and yoga. Any form of exercise is helpful, apart from those which require sudden bursts of high energy.

How often?

Older people should take some form of exercise on most days.

How intense?

Healthy exercise is never painful. Pain is a sign to stop, and chest pain is a particularly serious symptom, for which help should be sought immediately. However, exercise which does not cause any *discomfort* will not improve fitness, so the old person's aim should be to exercise to a degree that will cause a sensation of discomfort – a sensation that the body is working hard – but not to such an intensity that the exercise causes pain.

Examples of appropriate levels of discomfort are:

- breathlessness that interrupts an easy flow of speech, but does not make speech impossible
- an awareness of the heart beating
- the feeling that muscles and joints are being stretched.

How long?

Long enough to achieve discomfort – and then a few minutes longer. It is those extra few minutes of hard work which lead to an improvement in fitness – whether you are an Olympic athlete or eighty years old.

Health Checks – Are They Necessary?

In the 1960s there was great enthusiasm for 'screening' healthy old people, requiring them to perform tests in an attempt to identify disease at an early, symptomless, stage. There is no longer such enthusiasm for screening and most doctors now believe that old people who feel well do not have to have a lot of tests performed on them, at the time of retirement or at any other age.

There are, however, two groups of people who should be seen regularly – at least once a year, and more often if necessary.

1. People with chronic diseases, especially those who are receiving repeat medication.
2. Old people who have practical difficulties in asking their general

practitioner to visit if things are starting to go wrong; for example, people with dementia, or deafness, or blindness, or serious speech problems, and those who have no one to keep an eye on them and alert the general practitioner if any new problem develops.

It is unrealistic to expect a doctor or community nurse to call monthly on an old person whose condition is stable, but it is equally unrealistic for a general practitioner to issue one repeat prescription after another without ever seeing that old person. The service should be determined by the patient's condition and not by a set of rigid rules.

Good Food for Good Health

Many older people quite rightly consider they know a lot about food: as one person said, 'I've been eating for seventy-five years and survived.' This is true, but it is equally true that some nutritional problems do occur in old age.

Weight loss

Weight loss should be taken seriously. If a person sees a loss in weight when he mounts the scales, or notices that his clothes are loose, he should consult his general practitioner because weight loss may be an early sign of a serious disease.

Starvation and severe vitamin deficiencies are uncommon in old age. When they occur it is usually as a complication of some other problem, such as depression or dementia.

Obesity

Weight gain is more common than weight loss in old age. As at any age, it usually has a simple cause – the intake of more energy than is used in daily life. The remedy is the same at any age – an increase in energy expenditure (more exercise) and a decrease in energy intake (less food). This will tip the energy balance from weight gain to weight loss. Any of the good diet books, notably *The F Plan* by Audrey Eyton (Penguin Books, 1982), will help old people. This book is particularly good because it also helps counteract another common problem – that of fibre deficiency.

Fibre deficiency

Constipation owing to deficiency of fibre in the diet is a common cause of anxiety in old age. Although constipation does not have serious physical consequences, many old people regularly take laxatives because they believe that 'regularity' is essential for health. Old people are right to be worried and should consult the general practitioner if they notice any of the following:

- there is blood in the motion
- constipation alternates with diarrhoea
- there is a sudden change in bowel habit.

If, on the other hand, there is a gradual onset of constipation, the answer is more fibre – more roughage.

Remember also that a diet with fibre requires good teeth or good dentures.

Calcium deficiency

Recent research shows that many old people do not eat enough calcium, which is essential for strong and healthy bones.

Vitamin D deficiency often accompanies calcium deficiency, and it also contributes to bone disease in old age. Many house-bound people need Vitamin D, and the general practitioner or health visitor will advise on the best means of taking it. Old people who can get out and about can make their own Vitamin D by getting a suntan – simply on the forearms, face and neck – for the skin manufactures its own Vitamin D when it is bombarded with ultra-violet light. If an old person develops a well-tanned face and forearms in the summer, the Vitamin D that is made will last all winter until the summer sun comes back.

Alcohol

There is no reason why a person who has enjoyed a drink or two when working should not continue to do so in old age. Many people take less as they grow older, finding that a little bit less produces the same effects, but some people carry on without any change.

A small number of older people increase the amount they drink, and this can lead to trouble. The alcohol can cause a fall, or it can react with their prescribed drugs, or else it can lead to a general deterioration in their condition. People who become dependent on alcohol frequently try to hide this dependence from their family and friends, often successfully. Even housebound people can keep buying drink without their family or friends knowing, simply by phoning for a taxi to buy it and bring it to them.

When alcoholism develops in old people, it is usually possible to identify a cause – the death of a spouse or the loss of the ability to go out, for example. It is essential to try to tackle the problem at its root cause and not simply to stop the person from buying drink. This is very difficult for relatives to do, and help should be sought from a member of the primary care team (see p. 68).

Dental Care

Old people who still have their own teeth need regular visits to a dentist to keep them. It is also important to brush the teeth for three minutes twice a day, because this keeps the gums healthy – gum disease is the commonest reason for teeth falling out or being pulled out in middle and old age. The dentist can detect early signs of disease and give advice on the best way to brush the teeth.

The first set of dentures may have to be replaced after six months or so, because the gums shrink quickly in the months after the last teeth have been removed. After this the dentures should only need to be replaced every few years, when they become too loose. But if the gums become painful the advice of a dentist should be sought, whether or not the dentures feel loose.

Unfortunately, it is not always easy to find a dentist willing to offer National Health Service treatment. The best way of finding a good dentist is to ask friends who they use, but the best dentist is often the most popular, so you may not be able to find one this way. The next step is to look at an official list of local dentists. This is kept in the main post office and in libraries or at the Family Practitioner Committee. You will need to phone or visit the dentists on this list until you find one who is willing to offer NHS treatment.

Before starting a new course of treatment the old person should always check to ensure that the dentist agrees to give NHS treatment. All people receiving a supplementary pension are eligible for free treatment, as are some other old people who have a low income, even if their income is not so low as to qualify for a supplementary pension. If the old person's income is low, but not low enough for a supplementary pension, she should ask the dentist for Form FID, and take or post it to the local social security office to find out if she qualifies for free treatment. A charge is made for each set of dentures, except for those people who are eligible for free treatment, but everyone is entitled to free denture repairs.

DHSS leaflet DI I – *NHS dental treatment: what it costs and how to get free treatment* explains all these points in more detail. It should be available at your dentist's or at a local post office.

CHAPTER 3

Common Physical Problems

Certain health problems are common in old age. They are caused by disease in almost every case, because normal ageing does not cause serious health problems. However, it is not sufficient to tackle the problems simply by treating the disease which is the basic cause. Other steps must also be taken to deal with the disabilities and handicaps (see p. 15).

Difficulties with Self-care

To look after ourselves we need to be able to perform the following tasks:

- getting into and out of bed
- dressing and undressing
- getting to the toilet in time
- washing all over
- getting enough to eat and drink
- doing light housework.

If an old person loses the ability to do any of these things, she is at a disadvantage for three reasons.

1. She is dependent on other people and has to wait for their arrival before she can dress and go to the toilet.
2. She is at an increased risk of having to go into a home because

anything that affects her helpers – if, for example, the neighbour who prepares meals becomes ill – also affects her ability to live at home.

3. She feels dependent and a burden on others, although this does not bother all old people; some enjoy being looked after (see p. 90).

Problems with self-care rarely occur as a result of normal ageing. Usually they are caused by disease, complicated by the loss of strength, suppleness or skill that result from inactivity (see p. 19). Loss of the ability to get out of bed, or to dress, or to get into the bath may be the early signs of disease, and the general practitioner should be consulted. Most general practitioners now accept that the loss of the ability to function normally is as likely to be an early symptom of disease in old age as pain or bleeding, and that it must be taken as seriously as these symptoms. The general practitioner will therefore try to find the cause of the loss of functional ability, and any of the disabling diseases described in Chapter 4 may cause problems with self-care.

The general practitioner may refer the person with a problem in self-care to a geriatric out-patient clinic or day hospital, to be reviewed by a consultant in geriatric medicine. This is a doctor who has specialized in the care of old people and who has developed expertise in the management of the common problems of old age. He may also be able to solve problems that the general practitioner cannot deal with, because he works as a member of a team with nurses, occupational therapists and physiotherapists, and social workers.

The physiotherapist is trained to help old people to regain skills they have lost, either as a result of acute illness or over a long period of time, by showing them how to use their own skills and strengths to best advantage. For example, an elderly person who has difficulty walking develops bad habits: he struggles to pull himself out of his chair with his arms, and when walking shuffles along, bending forward in case he falls. The physiotherapist will show him how he can stand up more easily, for instance, by putting his feet near the front of the chair and moving his bottom well forward before trying to stand up. By demonstrating his bad posture and habits, perhaps with the use of a mirror, she can help him to regain the skill of walking upright, confidently and safely.

Unfortunately, few general practitioners have direct access to a physiotherapist's skills, or can ask a physiotherapist to visit a patient at home: most general practitioners have to refer people to a hospital clinic for physiotherapy. Physiotherapy can also be obtained privately, through the *Yellow Pages*. If you choose a physiotherapist with MCSP or SRP after her name, you can be confident that she is well qualified. Private physiotherapy can, however, be expensive, and it is wise to ask the general practitioner if he thinks physiotherapy is necessary, or whether NHS physiotherapy is available, before arranging for private treatment.

The job of the occupational therapist is to help an individual who has suffered some physical impairment – owing to weakness and stiffness for example – to cope with that impairment, so that it has the least possible impact on her life. The occupational therapist's first step is to try to teach the person how she can overcome her difficulty. For example, most people who have had a stroke find dressing easier if the weak arm is put in a sleeve first, but not everyone finds this sort of thing out for themself, and the occupational therapist is able to pass on many such tips. If this fails she may provide an aid. This could be a bath seat, for instance, for a person who finds it very difficult to stand up again once he has sat down on the bottom of the bath. Sometimes the occupational therapist has to help the person with a disability to adapt her home, if the provision of advice and aids is ineffective. The types of adaptation that can be undertaken if financial help is provided are as numerous as the types of disability, but the following are examples of common adaptations:

- the installation of a stairlift if the only toilet is upstairs
- the construction of a downstairs toilet and shower if the stairs are not suitable for a stairlift
- the conversion of two steps at the front door to a ramp that allows a person in a wheelchair to leave his home.

Important though such practical changes may be, the ability of the occupational therapist or physiotherapist to restore the disabled person's confidence to overcome his disability is one of the most important skills, because loss of confidence is just as great a problem as loss of physical ability.

The advice of an occupational therapist is usually easier to obtain than the advice of a physiotherapist. Most occupational therapists work in hospital, although some – known as domiciliary occupational therapists – work outside hospital. They can be contacted by writing to or phoning the local social services department, or by asking the general practitioner, health visitor or district nurse.

Immobility

Immobility may result in the elderly person becoming housebound or unable to reach the upstairs of her house or, at the worst, becoming confined to one room or even her chair.

Early signs

Loss of the ability to do something which the old person could once do with ease; for example, walking to the shops or to the pub, or the onset of difficulty in climbing stairs may be a sign.

Common causes

- arthritis
- Parkinson's disease
- visual impairments
- stroke
- loss of fitness (either on its own or as a complication of one of the other diseases).

Primary care

The general practitioner will try to find the cause of the loss of mobility, if necessary referring the person to a hospital clinic. If the immobility is due to arthritis or stroke she may try to arrange physiotherapy, or for the provision of a walking stick or zimmer aid. (This is a frame with four feet which the old person can use as an aid to walking.) If nothing can be done to improve mobility, a wheelchair may be necessary – either one to use outside the house or one for the old person to use most of the time inside the house. It is unwise for relatives to provide a zimmer frame or a wheelchair before they have sought professional advice – such aids should only be resorted to when attempts to treat the underlying disease have been unsuccessful in restoring mobility.

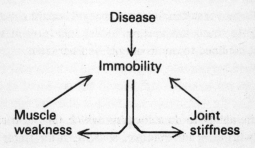

What can the old person do?

Keep active: immobility is in a vicious circle which starts with the loss of fitness. If the general practitioner says it is safe to do so, the affected person should set a goal for himself every day; for example, trying each day to walk down the road one gate further.

What can relatives and helpers do?

Encourage the old person to keep active; help her plan her walking programme and take her to interesting places to walk.

Foot Problems

Many old people are immobilized not by rare and serious diseases but by one most common problem – painful feet.

Cutting toenails

Some old people simply find difficulty in cutting their toenails because they cannot bend to reach them, or because their eyes are too poor to see them. These people need someone to cut their nails for them. Nails should be cut straight across; sharp corners which cut into the neighbouring flesh should be rounded with a file, and thick horny toenails should be filed down with a file or board rubbed horizontally across the nail to reduce its thickness. Anyone can cut toenails, and should feel confident in doing so, provided that the old person has neither diabetes nor peripheral vascular disease. These two diseases make the skin of the feet very susceptible to injury and infection, so foot care for people suffering from them should be provided by a qualified chiropodist.

If you do not live near enough to cut the elderly person's toenails regularly, you can either refer him to a chiropodist or, if he is already receiving district nursing, ask the district nurse to do it for him while she is providing other aspects of nursing care.

Painful feet

If the cause of pain is a corn, the chiropodist should be consulted. An old person with a corn should not attack it with a knife or razor blade. Few lesions are easier to cause or more difficult to heal than an ulcer on the foot.

If the person is suffering from generalized pain in the foot he should also consult a chiropodist, provided that he has not developed the pain as the result of an injury or accident. If this is possibly the cause, an X-ray will be necessary in case a bone has been fractured. However, pain in the foot is usually a chronic problem caused by osteoarthritis in the small joints of the foot, and it can often be relieved by shoe inserts of the correct design and placement.

Finding a chiropodist

The N H S chiropody service is in very short supply, but you should always apply to it before considering private treatment. Ask at the health centre or surgery how best to proceed, and ask for a doctor's letter if the old person has diabetes or peripheral vascular disease, or if immobility is adversely affecting his health. The *Yellow Pages* list many chiropodists offering private treatment: choose one who has the letters S.R.Ch. after her name, meaning State Registered Chiropodist, for assurance that she is well qualified.

Incontinence

Incontinence can be due to disease of the bladder and the tissues round the bladder, or it can occur as a complication of dementia or stroke. In this chapter only the former type of incontinence is discussed: see p. 85 for discussion of incontinence resulting from dementia or stroke.

Urinary Incontinence in Men

Early signs

- difficulty in starting to pass water
- dribbling at the end of passing water
- need to pass water frequently
- inability to wait once the need 'to go' is felt.

Common causes

Swelling of the prostate gland is the most common cause of urinary incontinence in men. It is not a sign of cancer of the prostate. Loss of control of the bladder may occur as one complication of a severe stroke (see p. 53).

Primary care

The general practitioner should be consulted. If he suspects prostate enlargement, he may refer the old man to a urological surgeon, although he may not do so immediately if the problem is at an early stage. Surgery of the prostate is safe and effective. It does not cause incontinence or sexual impotence.

If the incontinence is the result of a stroke the general practitioner will treat it in the same way as incontinence resulting from dementia.

What can the old person do?

Tell other people about the problem early: sometimes shame leads the sufferer to hide his problem. Avoid constipation (see p. 23).

What can relatives do?

Ensure that the person can reach the toilet in time once he feels the need to go. Inability to hold one's water, combined with immobility, can result in incontinence *en route* to the toilet. If in doubt provide a chamber pot or a 'bottle', which can be obtained in a pharmacy or from the district nurse. A bottle is always useful for use at night: keep it beside the bed and provide a light that can be reached easily from the bed.

Urinary Incontinence in Women

Early signs

The first sign often occurs in middle age when the woman notices that some urine, perhaps not very much at first, is passed when she coughs or laughs or tries to run.

Common causes

The most common cause is the effect of childbirth on the muscles which line the pelvis and control the flow of urine at the lower end of the bladder. These muscles can become stretched during pregnancy and delivery, and if strength is not recovered in the months and years after birth, control of the flow of urine is progressively lost, and what is called 'stress incontinence' develops. If the affected person also develops an infection of the bladder the symptoms become even worse. Constipation can also aggravate incontinence of urine.

Primary care

If an old person develops stress incontinence, or if it becomes more than she can cope with by simple measures such as the use of a sanitary towel to keep herself dry, she should see her general practitioner. If there is infection, it can be treated. If no infection is present, the general practitioner may ask the district nurse to teach the patient how to try to regain control. One way is for the person to try to stop the flow of urine three times every time she passes water, but there are other exercises which can be helpful. If the problem is severe, or if stress incontinence is accompanied by a prolapse of loose tissue, the general practitioner may refer the sufferer to a gynaecologist.

What can the old person do?

There are exercises which can help her to regain control of the flow of urine. If these are unsuccessful, the old person may have to use pads to absorb the flow of urine: ask the district nurse for advice.

What can relatives do?

Help the sufferer to seek help: too often older people regard this type of problem as something that must be accepted.

Faecal Incontinence

Early signs

Soiled underpants, nightdress and sheets. Some disabled people give the appearance of faecal incontinence when the problem is simply either that they cannot reach their bottom to wipe it, or that they cannot see well enough to know whether they have wiped well or not.

Common causes

The commonest cause in people who do not have dementia or a stroke is constipation. The bowel becomes packed with hard faeces, and fluid faeces leak past the obstructing lumps.

What can the old person do?

Eating more fibre (see p. 23) is a help, but the sufferer should be careful and increase his fibre intake slowly. A sudden large increase in fibre intake can have explosive results.

Avoid laxatives.

What can relatives do?

Point out to their elderly relative that he is having problems if they notice soiled underpants or smears of faeces on the toilet seat, and help him to modify his diet.

Primary care

If the problem persists for another two weeks after you have tried to help, seek the advice of the general practitioner or district nurse. If a person is severely constipated he may require one, or more than one, enema to clear the bowels.

If the old person complains of severe pain, or if blood or mucus is noticed, the general practitioner should be contacted as soon as possible.

Dizziness and Loss of Balance

Early symptoms

- staggering or falling when standing up or when turning the neck
- a fall not preceded by a trip
- a blackout

Common causes

There are many possible causes of blackouts. The commonest are abnormalities in the heart rhythm, and temporary blockage of blood flow to the brain.

If an old person simply feels dizzy, but does not stagger or fall, there is less likely to be a serious cause.

If the main problem is a feeling that the room is swinging round, together with vomiting, the person is said to have vertigo. One common cause of vertigo is Ménière's syndrome.

Some drugs can also cause this sensation.

Primary care

The general practitioner should be contacted if an old person has a blackout or a fall without any obvious cause, or if she becomes too anxious to leave the house or walk without grabbing on to the furniture for fear of falling.

What can the old person do?

Not very much, unfortunately, except to try to keep calm and to avoid leaning forward when walking, as this will make her even more unsteady.

What can relatives do?

Provide comfort and support for the person afflicted with what can be a dreadful condition.

Visual Impairment

The lens of the eye becomes less elastic with age, and this often means that you need to change the strength of your lenses. For this reason, it is wise for an older person to visit an optician every two years to have his vision tested, even though he may not have noticed any change since he last had it tested. Everyone is entitled to a free NHS sight test either by an ophthalmic optician or an ophthalmic medical practitioner, and if new glasses are needed both the lenses and the frame can be provided free, if the old person receives a supplementary pension. Some old people who are not so poor as to qualify for a supplementary pension, but who have a low income, may also qualify for free glasses. An old person who is warned about the cost of NHS glasses should ask for form FI and send it to the local social security office. DHSS Form GII – *NHS Glasses: how much they cost and how to get them free* – which can be obtained at post offices, describes these arrangements in more detail.

If a person notices that he is seeing less well than formerly, he should of course seek advice right away, even though it is less than two years since he last saw his optician.

If an eye becomes red and painful, the old person should go, or be taken, to his general practitioner or to the casualty department of the local eye hospital as soon as possible. If the vision has started to fail slowly and painlessly, it is appropriate to go to the optician in the first instance. All that may be needed is a change of spectacle lenses, but the optician is trained to detect disease if it is developing. This is one important reason why older people are better advised to go to an optician when they think they need glasses, and not simply to buy a new pair from a department store which does not have an optician.

The changes that occur as a result of normal ageing do not cause blindness, or even significant loss of vision. It is only when disease develops that a serious loss of vision occurs. There are three common types of eye disease in old age:

- cataract
- glaucoma
- senile macular degeneration.

Cataract

In cataract the lens of one or both eyes becomes cloudy. Usually one eye is affected more than the other. In most cases it is not possible to identify any cause.

Common symptoms

Gradual loss of vision, which is often attributed to 'old age' or the need for new spectacles.

What can the sufferer do?

Consult an optician as soon as sight starts to fail. Not only is an accurate diagnosis important, but the provision of the right type of lenses can improve vision even when a person has cataract. An eye-shield to protect the eyes from the direct glare of light is often very helpful.

What can the family do?

Help the old person improve her domestic lighting. A person with cataract needs bright light focused on her book or working place, whereas many older people depend on a weak bulb dangling in the middle of the room; useful gifts are:

- 100 watt bulbs
- reading lights for bedroom, kitchen and living-room
- a standard lamp to place beside a favourite chair.

Primary care

The general practitioner can refer the old person to an ophthalmologist, who will remove the lens if he thinks the person might benefit.

Glaucoma

In this disease damage is caused by a steady increase in the pressure inside the eye. The cause is unknown.

Early symptoms

In the early stages glaucoma is symptomless. It is painless and does not cause noticeable loss of vision until a very late stage. The fact that glaucoma is a symptomless disease is one of the reasons why an old person should have his eyes checked every two years, since it may be diagnosed by the optician in the course of a routine sight test.

Primary care

The general practitioner usually refers the old person to the eye hospital for assessment. The treatment consists of eye drops.

What can the sufferer do?

Remember to put in the eye drops regularly. Seek help immediately if the eye becomes painful or red.

What can relatives do?

Ensure that treatment is taken regularly, and encourage and support the old person. Glaucoma rarely leads to complete blindness. In most cases the old person is left with some useful vision. Although the ophthalmologist will tell the old person this, a fear of blindness is understandably one which can recur, and the person may require repeated reassurance.

Senile Macular Degeneration

The cause of this disease is not known. A common early sign is difficulty with reading. Unlike sight change from normal causes, the loss of vision is progressive. The result is that the person may lose the power to read or sew, even with glasses. However, this disease rarely results in complete blindness, and the person is usually left with enough vision to get about the house safely.

Coping with Blindness

Even after the best treatment, the affected person may still be very disabled by his poor vision.

If ordinary glasses do not allow the person to read a book or paper, he may still be able to do so, given the right type of aid. For example, a magnifying glass with a light attached may help. These can be found easily, but shop around before buying one, as the price varies. Low-vision aids are also supplied by the NHS, and if an old person is attending an eye hospital he should be given advice about the best type of vision aid.

Social services departments employ staff who can help a blind person to regain the confidence to walk outside and to care for himself again. If the old person is attending a clinic in an eye hospital he should ask for an appointment with the medical social worker. If this is not possible he should phone or write to the social worker for the blind at the local social services department. He should also contact the local Association for the Blind, which is listed under 'Blind' in the telephone directory.

Hearing Problems

One of the effects of normal ageing is to reduce the ears' ability to hear high notes. This does not, however, result in any serious handicap, and for most people the most noticeable effect is increasing difficulty in hearing the telephone ring. If someone is unable to hear normal speech, or requests the television to be turned up so loud that others complain, the general practitioner should be consulted. Wax in the ears is a common curable cause of deafness, but if no cause for the loss of hearing can be detected the general practitioner will consider referral to an ear, nose and throat specialist – provided the loss of hearing is distressing or disabling the old person.

A hearing aid will help some people, but it is important that a person who is developing hearing difficulties should not immediately go and buy a hearing aid. The *Yellow Pages* list a number of hearing-aid suppliers and dispensers, but before purchasing an aid privately the person with a hearing problem should try an NHS hearing aid, and take the advice of one of the staff at the hearing-aid clinic. There are, in addition, a number of aids that can help a deaf person – for example, a telephone that can be amplified, or a light which flashes when the door bell is rung. Advice on these and other aids can be obtained from the social worker for the deaf at the social services department, or from the local centre for the deaf and hard of hearing. Look under 'Deaf' in the telephone directory to find the address and telephone number of your nearest centre.

You can do a lot to help someone who is hard of hearing.

- Do not shout: speaking slowly is more important than speaking in a loud voice.
- Do not contort your face in an attempt to help the deaf person lipread. Do not eat or smoke while speaking.
- Do let the person see your face: let light shine on it if possible rather than sitting with your back to the light. Encourage the deaf person to wear her spectacles so that she can see your face clearly.
- Do turn off the radio or television to cut down background noise.

Finally, do remember how depressing deafness, or even the fear of deafness, can be and give comfort and support to someone with hearing loss.

Speech Problems

The most common cause of speech problems is a stroke. This may result in a loss of the sufferers' ability to understand the meaning of the words spoken to them, or an inability to find the correct words when speaking, or both. Sometimes the person also has difficulty in pronouncing clearly any words that she does say, because her facial muscles are weak. The result can be confusing for an old person's family – and frustrating for her if, for example, she can only reply, 'Yes, yes, yes, yes,' to a question. A stroke can by itself cause a person's mood to swing from happiness to tears: if speech problems are also present, attempts to hold a conversation may frequently finish in tears because the old person is often aware that she is not finding the correct words. This leads to a vicious circle, because the more upset a person is by her speech problem the worse the speech problem becomes.

You can help someone to recover the power of speech by encouraging them to talk, particularly if you follow these tips.

- Do not try to provide a missing word or guess what the person is saying as soon as she hesitates or makes a mistake: sit back, keep calm and give encouraging nods.
- Speak slowly and clearly, and let the affected person speak slowly too: hurry and tension always make things worse.
- Encourage the affected person to sing hymns and songs of childhood: these sometimes come out easily.
- Remember that badly fitting dentures aggravate speech problems.
- Make allowances if the old person is deaf.

Finally, remember – and remind others – that the old person may be able to understand other people, even though she cannot speak, and she should therefore not be spoken to like a child or spoken about as if she were not there.

The general practitioner can refer a person with serious speech problems to a hospital clinic to see a speech therapist, but the greatest need of many people with speech problems is simply conversation and communication.

Hypothermia

Hypothermia is a serious condition in which the body temperature drops below the normal minimum level. It can be fatal. It is most common among elderly people, for a number of reasons.

1. An older person does not detect a drop in environmental temperature.
2. An older person does not react normally to a decrease in temperature. Instead of the normal reaction, such as shivering, the body makes no reaction and continues to lose heat.
3. Some old people have a low income and find heating expensive.
4. Many old people live in houses which are expensive and difficult to heat.
5. Some old people, even if they have money, are very reluctant to use the heating that they have. This is in part because they are afraid of debt and in part because they have always been used to a cold house.

Some groups are particularly at risk, for example those with thyroid deficiency or those who are taking barbiturates or phenothiazine drugs.

Prevention

You can take a number of steps to reduce the risk of hypothermia.

1. Help the old person to claim all the allowances for which she is eligible, so that she has enough money to provide heat.
2. Help make the house draught-free; insulate the loft, lag the hot water tank, and line the curtains. Some old people double-glaze the window in the room in which they spend most of their time, and this is a good step to take, even though it is expensive.
3. Help the old person to develop an efficient heating system. Outdated radiant fires are expensive to run. In general, the older the heating apparatus, the less efficient and more expensive it will be. Elderly people who are too disabled to manage their existing heating apparatus, perhaps because their arthritis is too bad for them to carry coal, can be helped with a grant to put in new appliances which they can manage better, for example gas fires. You should ask the domiciliary occupational therapist for advice. Often a charity such as the Regimental Fund, or the welfare fund of the old person's former employers will be able to help with a lump sum. Some people can clearly see what needs to be done but cannot afford to do it.
4. Encourage the old person to wear warm clothing.
5. Encourage her to have warm food and drink in cold weather.
6. Encourage her to keep active.

Recognition and treatment

Hypothermia may be difficult to recognize. Usually the elderly person is drowsy and looks unwell, but in some cases the face may be flushed.

If a part of the body which is covered by clothes feels cold – for example the forearm or back or the abdominal wall – then hypothermia should be suspected and action taken. If you suspect hypothermia, phone the general practitioner or the district nurse as soon as you can. Put extra clothes round her and increase the heat in the room, but be careful not to point a source of radiant heat, such as an electric fire, directly at her. Hot food and drink will be helpful, but if she is drowsy do not attempt to give anything by mouth.

Preparing for a fall

Some elderly people develop hypothermia because they have fallen and lain on the floor. Try to ensure that the whole house is warm, for example by installing a gas convector heater in the hall. Devise a means by which she can contact a neighbour or yourself if she should fall.

Keeping warm in bed

Some elderly people are reluctant to heat their bedrooms, and particular attention must be paid to this. It is essential to heat an old person's bedroom before she goes to bed, even though she may always have gone to bed without heating, and even with an open window, when she was younger. An electric over-blanket with a safety switch is a good and safe solution.

Problems with Drugs and Medicines

Old people are more sensitive to the effects of drugs than younger people. They suffer from side-effects more easily, and doctors now attempt to prevent drug-induced disease by prescribing

- as few drugs as possible
- as low a dosage as possible
- as simple a routine as possible.

In addition, doctors now take more care when prescribing to listen to what the old person has to say about her drugs, and then to tell the old person –

1. What the drug will do.
2. Why it is important for her.
3. How often and how long to take it.
4. What side-effects to watch out for.
5. When to come back and see the doctor again.

This is particularly important for older people with memory problems, because the old person who makes mistakes with her medicines is at even higher risk of side-effects. Mistakes with medicines are common when the old person is started on a new drug, or when she is discharged from hospital with a whole set of new drugs, but still has all the medicines she was taking before admission in the bathroom cabinet.

What can relatives do?

The first step is to find out the information listed in points 1 to 5 in the previous section, so that you know why the medicines have been prescribed. The pharmacist who dispenses the medicines is in an ideal position to provide information on the first four points, but will not know the doctor's plans for reviewing the medication.

This type of information is helpful, but it does not necessarily ensure that the old person will take the medicines as the doctor intended. Some people know all about their medicines but forget to take them, while others know nothing except that they have to take 'two white and a yellow every morning', and manage to do that perfectly.

A good routine is of great importance. If the old person does not have a routine, the second step is to encourage him to develop one. The simplest approach is to keep the medicine beside the razor or the tea caddy or the toothpaste, or whatever will be used at the time the pills are meant to be taken. The pharmacist who dispensed the pills is a very useful source of advice if you are wondering if two or three tablets can be taken all together, or if the medicines should be taken before, with or after food. If the old person has memory failure, someone else may have to put out his pills – in one, or more than one, egg cup – not only to help him to remember to take them but also to allow you or his helpers to check that he has taken them.

The third step which relatives can take is to ensure that the old person consults his general practitioner if he thinks that the medicine is making him unwell, or if he stops taking the pills. Side-effects are common and should be reported, but the therapeutic effects – the good effects – of medicines are also important, and if an old person stops taking his medicine his condition may get worse. Old people sometimes stop taking pills which they think are making them unwell, when the symptoms they are feeling have nothing at all to do with their medicines. It is also very important to report mistakes to the general practitioner. He may be able to simplify the combination of drugs he is prescribing or perhaps even stop some of them altogether.

Self-medication

Old people consume a great many medicines that they buy over the counter without prescription. By and large self-medication does no harm. The only form of self-medication which causes many problems is the over-use of laxatives (see p. 23). Furthermore, old people should be encouraged to use the old-fashioned family remedies they have used for years – remedies such as hot toddy or hot lemon drinks. They make the old person feel good and do no harm, which cannot be said for all modern medicines.

CHAPTER 4

Common Physical Diseases

A small number of physical diseases are responsible for the majority of the disabilities which are found in old age. In this chapter the contribution that the affected person and his family can make to the care of each of these important diseases is described, but there are some general points about self-care and family care which need to be emphasized.

Self-care is the most important form of care, and the ability of a sufferer to care for himself is determined not only by the degree of his disability but also by the nature of his reaction to his illness. Everyone reacts in his own way, but certain types of reaction are commonly encountered.

Depression – 'It's terrible, I just cry all the time.'
Bitterness – and anger – 'Why me, why did it happen to me?'
Hopelessness – 'what's the use of trying at my age?'

For most people these are only temporary phases before they adapt to their new condition by accepting it, and then by fighting to overcome the problems which the disease causes. The speed with which an individual adapts depends in part upon the type and severity of his illness, but even more important factors are his personality and the reaction of other people to his illness. Some people cope much better with illness in old age than others, and this often reflects a lifelong ability to cope with setbacks and adversity with determination and good humour. However, even the most resilient person can fall into depression if those around him are depressed and pessimistic.

Someone who becomes disabled obviously needs sympathy and support, but it is not particularly helpful if:

- the sympathy is always accompanied by a gloomy or serious expression
- relatives talk about nothing else but the illness
- all decisions are made for the ill person
- all tasks are taken away from the ill person, denying him the opportunity to do anything for himself or – even more important – for other people.

Stroke

Common causes

A stroke is caused when an artery in the brain becomes blocked, or bursts open with bleeding into the brain tissue. Whatever the cause, the effect is the same – deprivation of oxygen from the part of the brain supplied by that artery. People who have a stroke often have some other disease of the arteries, for example ischaemic heart disease (see p. 55) or high blood pressure.

Common consequences

The effects depend upon which part of the brain is affected. The most common effect is a weakness or complete paralysis of one side of the body, accompanied by a loss of sensation. The sufferer cannot feel the affected side of the body, and may also have great difficulty in knowing the position of the affected limb if she is unable to see it. Furthermore, a stroke may affect the individual's ability to see all round: she may have large blind spots. Speech may be affected, most commonly the ability to say what is desired; for example, the affected person may want to answer a question but is only able to say 'yes, yes, yes, yes, yes'. This is a source of great frustration.

Almost always the sufferer makes a significant improvement in the months following a stroke.

What can the sufferer do?

Keep active: exercising the paralysed part of her body as much as possible, using the unaffected side to do so. Stiffness is a major problem after a stroke, and if the affected side can be kept supple, the eventual outcome will be much better.

What can the family do?

Keep calm and hopeful. Few diseases have a more shattering impact on the affected person and his family than stroke, and the sufferer may become very depressed and easily plunged into tearful despondency.

The family can help the sufferer to exercise.

Primary care

The general practitioner has to make an accurate diagnosis of the cause of the stroke, but there are no specific treatments available to minimize brain damage. The contribution of the general practitioner and district nurse is therefore primarily to advise the sufferer and her family on the steps they can take to promote recovery.

The district nurse can also provide help with bathing and self-care in the early days when disability is at a maximum.

Physiotherapy is often helpful, if it can be arranged.

Hospital care

Where it is possible, home care is best, but hospital admission may be necessary to diagnose the cause of the stroke or to provide more nursing care than can be given at home.

Outlook

Fairly hopeful: most survivors regain more abilities than seems possible immediately after the stroke, and many do not get further strokes after the first.

Heart Disease

Common causes

There are two common causes:

1. Rheumatic fever in childhood.
2. Narrowing of the arteries which supply the heart muscle with oxygen (ischaemic heart disease).

The second cause itself stems from:

- cigarette smoking
- high blood pressure
- high levels of fat in the blood.

Common consequences

1. Chest pain on exercise (angina) relieved by rest.
2. Acute, severe chest pain – a heart attack (myocardial infarction).

3. Blackouts, caused by an irregular heart rhythm.
4. Breathlessness and swollen ankles caused by heart failure.

What can the sufferer do?

- lose weight if obese
- take medicines as prescribed and report any new symptom quickly
- take gentle exercise

What can the family do?

- help the sufferer lose weight
- encourage gentle exercise

Primary care

The general practitioner can:

- prescribe drugs to relieve angina
- prescribe drugs, usually digoxin and a diuretic (water pill), for heart failure.

Hospital care

Hospital care may be necessary if the person becomes acutely ill, for example with a heart attack. Or it might be for:

- insertion of a pacemaker to prevent blackouts
- coronary artery bypass grafting to relieve angina, by helping blood flow past narrowed segments of the arteries which supply the heart muscle.

Outlook

Good, with the right treatment.

Many people live well for years after their first heart attack. Severe disability is uncommon, but limitation in mobility due to angina or breathlessness restricts a number of sufferers to their house and garden.

Further information

You can find out more from the Chest, Heart and Stroke Association (see p. 161).

Peripheral Vascular Disease

Common causes

Narrowing of the arteries taking oxygen-rich blood to the lower limbs. The main factors leading to this are:

- cigarette smoking
- diabetes.

Common consequences

- pain in one calf or thigh that develops while the person is walking and is relieved by rest
- an ulcer on the foot or heel that fails to heal
- reddening of skin of one or more toes or of the heel

What can the sufferer do?

- stop smoking
- keep active
- keep the feet warm
- ask a chiropodist to cut nails and treat corns

What can the family do?

Help the person to stop smoking.

Primary care

General practitioners have no effective drugs for this disease but they can:

- give advice on foot care
- help the person stop smoking
- treat the diabetes effectively
- refer the sufferer for chiropody.

The district nurse can:

- give advice on foot care
- treat any cuts or ulcers.

Hospital care

This is necessary if gangrene develops or if there is severe disabling pain.

Surgical treatment of the narrowed arteries may be effective, but amputation is sometimes required.

Outlook

Fairly hopeful: in a significant proportion of cases, the symptoms either improve or stay the same. The outlook is much improved if the sufferer can stop smoking.

Parkinson's Disease

Common causes

In some cases the disease is a late complication of the 1919 'sleeping sickness' epidemic, but many cases have no identifiable cause.

Common consequences

- stiffness
- tremor, particularly a shaking of the hands
- difficulties with writing
- shuffling steps
- slowness of movement
- difficulties in swallowing

What can the sufferer do?

Take the treatment as it is prescribed. Report any new symptoms quickly.

What can the family do?

- encourage the sufferer to keep meeting other people, even though his appearance has been altered and he feels shy
- join the Parkinson's Disease Society

Primary care

The tasks of the general practitioner are:

- accurate diagnosis
- referral to a neurologist or consultant in geriatric medicine
- treatment, usually with one of the drugs derived from L-dopa.

Hospital care

Usually out-patient only; in-patient care may be arranged if further investigation is necessary or if a change of treatment is necessary.

Outlook

Only a small proportion of people become severely disabled by Parkinson's disease. The outlook is brighter if the patient makes a good response to drug treatment.

Further information

You can find out more from the Parkinson's Disease Society (see p. 163).

Bronchitis and Emphysema

Common causes

- cigarette smoking
- air pollution
- industrial dusts

Common consequences

- breathlessness
- coughing and spitting
- wheezing

What can the sufferer do?

- stop smoking
- keep active
- seek help early if condition deteriorates – if, for example, breathlessness increases or sputum turns green

What can the family do?

- help the sufferer to stop smoking
- remain calm during a wheezy or breathless attack; tension makes breathlessness worse

Primary care

The general practitioner can:

- give advice on stopping smoking
- prescribe antibiotics for the acute infections which complicate chronic bronchitis from time to time
- prescribe drugs for the asthma which may complicate bronchitis
- offer immunization against influenza if appropriate
- arrange physiotherapy if there is a domiciliary physiotherapy service in his area.

Hospital care

This may be necessary during an acute infection, because breathlessness is usually aggravated and heart failure may result from the fact that the heart has to do even more work than usual. The hospital consultant may, in discussion with the general practitioner, arrange for the sufferer to have oxygen cylinders in his home.

Outlook

In only a small proportion of cases does the sufferer become housebound because of bronchitis. Outlook is improved if the sufferer can stop smoking.

Arthritis

Causes

There are two common types of arthritis – rheumatoid arthritis and osteoarthritis. The latter may affect a single joint (a hip or a knee) or be widespread, affecting the spinal column and the small joints of hand and foot. Where one joint is severely affected the cause is usually some past injury to that joint, for example an infection that took place in childhood. The cause of rheumatoid arthritis is not known; the joints are clearly inflamed, but they are not infected.

Common consequences

Pain and stiffness, often affecting the small joints of the hands and feet.

What can the sufferer do?

Keep active. This is often very difficult because of the pain, but one of the main objectives of treatment is to control pain in order to allow movement, and so prevent further loss of suppleness in the joints and of strength in the muscles that move the joint.

What can the family do?

The family should try not to do much. Relatives must be careful that they do not take over tasks that the sufferer could do for herself because they feel anxious about her condition or distressed by her discomfort and pain.

Primary care

The general practitioner may prescribe drugs to combat the inflammation and to control the pain. Sometimes more than one drug is necessary. The domiciliary occupational therapist (see p. 30) can advise if disabilities develop.

The District Nursing Service can help with bathing if the affected person loses the ability to bath or wash herself all over.

Hospital care

Physiotherapy is usually provided by a hospital service, for few parts of the country have a domiciliary physiotherapy service.

Admission may be necessary for investigation or to allow drug treatment to be altered.

Surgical replacement of affected joints may be possible in severe cases.

Outlook

Reasonably good: only a very small proportion of sufferers finish up confined to a wheelchair, although this is a very common fear when the diagnosis is first made.

Diabetes

Common causes

Obesity is the commonest cause when diabetes starts in old age. Usually no cause can be identified in the case of people who become diabetic in childhood or early adult life.

Common consequences

In diabetes the concentration of sugar – and of many other chemicals – in the bloodstream varies to a much greater degree than it would normally. High sugar (glucose) concentrations can lead to coma, low sugar concentrations to blackouts and fainting.

People with diabetes are at higher risk of heart disease, stroke and peripheral vascular disease than others. They are also prone to infections.

What can the sufferer do?

- lose weight, if overweight, by eating a diet low in refined carbohydrate, glucose or sucrose (table sugar) and fat, but high in fibre
- seek help early if an infection, such as a boil or urinary tract infection, develops
- ask a chiropodist to cut toenails and treat corns, because there

is a high risk of infection and ulceration if the skin of the foot is cut
- the person with diabetes is also expected to monitor his own care, for example by regular urine tests

What can the family do?

Help the sufferer lose weight.

Primary care

The general practitioner can:

- give advice on weight loss and diet
- prescribe treatment; insulin is rarely necessary if diabetes develops in old age, and treatment is usually in tablet form.

The health visitor can also be a useful source of advice.

Hospital care

The general practitioner may request a second opinion if the first treatment he tries is ineffective.

The dietitian at the hospital clinic is an excellent source of advice on diet.

Outlook

Reasonably good, provided the diabetes is well controlled.

Further information

The British Diabetic Association publishes many leaflets and booklets. It also has local branches which provide information and support for people with newly diagnosed diabetes and for their families.

Cancer

Common causes

Ageing does not cause cancer. Cancers are more common in old age because older people have been exposed to the factors which do cause cancer for a longer period of time. The most important of these factors is cigarette smoking, which accounts for about one-third of cancers.

Excessive exposure to sunlight is a cause of one type of skin cancer.

Common symptoms

There are so many different types of cancer that early symptoms vary greatly. However, certain symptoms are common, and early advice should be sought from the general practitioner if they are present.

- any ulcer or sore on the lip or skin which fails to heal
- coughing up blood or bloody sputum
- weight loss
- passage of blood in the motions, or alternating diarrhoea and constipation
- the growth of a lump

What can the sufferer do?

The most important step that an old person can take is to report any of the symptoms listed above quickly.

Stopping smoking is probably also effective in reducing risk.

What can the family do?

Families can help by encouraging the sufferer to take a positive outlook on life, because the outlook is better than many people think.

Primary care

The general practitioner's main responsibility is to diagnose or suspect cancer and refer the patient to hospital if necessary.

The community nursing service is of vital importance in the provision of good terminal care.

Outlook

To many people the diagnosis 'cancer' sounds like a death sentence. This is not the case. Some cancers are curable, and none of them is untreatable. The control of pain and other symptoms is now very much better than it was.

CHAPTER 5

The Main Sources of Practical Help

There are many sources of help, but simply to describe these sources is not enough, for even if you know about the services which should exist, two problems are common – difficulty in obtaining the service that is needed and complaints about the service that is given.

Primary Care

The general practitioner

An old person's general practitioner can do much to help her and her family. His main contribution is the treatment of acute and chronic disease, but if he has been her general practitioner for many years his advice and friendship will also be valued by the old person when she is considering important decisions, such as whether or not to move house.

Few general practitioners now pay monthly visits to housebound people, because most believe that their time is better spent on those old people who have acute or chronic medical problems – for example an old person who has just been prescribed two different drugs. Most general practitioners continue to be interested in the home conditions of their elderly patients, but nowadays the majority of them work as members of primary care teams with district nurses and health visitors. If one of the team is visiting the home of an old person, the general practitioner will be well informed about the conditions there and will therefore not need to visit himself.

If an old person is acutely ill it is reasonable to ask the general practitioner to visit her at home. If the receptionist tries to persuade you that the old person could come to the surgery, simply ask to speak directly to the doctor and be politely persistent until you can request a home visit directly.

If the old person wishes to change her general practitioner you should help her with these three steps:

1. Find the name of another general practitioner; ask around her friends and acquaintances for the name of a good one.
2. Write to that general practitioner, asking if he will accept the old person as a patient. An explanation of the reason for wanting to change will be helpful, but is not necessary.
3. If the general practitioner is willing to accept the person on to his list, either inform the receptionist (in writing or in person) at the surgery where she is currently registered, or else write directly to the Family Practitioner Committee for the area in which the old person lives, and ask them to arrange the transfer.

One important point is to emphasize to old people that they must be honest with their general practitioner. If he has prescribed medicine that does not appear to be doing good, or actually appears to be causing harm, the old person must say so, for the general practitioner cannot work without the relevant information.

The district nurse

The district nursing service is staffed by two types of nurse:

- the State Registered District Nurse, who performs skilled tasks such as insulin injections or the treatment of bed sores

- the care assistant (nursing auxiliary) whose time is spent in helping people with their personal care – for example with bathing or with using the commode.

In many parts of the country it is possible for a severely disabled person who needs skilled treatment, or who has no one else to help with personal care, to receive help seven days a week, sometimes more than once a day. In some parts of the country nurses also make visits in the evening, usually to people who need essential treatments such as an injection of a pain-killing drug to help them through the night. In a few places night nursing is available, although it is usually only possible to arrange night care for cancer patients, because certain of the cancer charities are willing to pay for night sitting if the district nursing service can arrange it.

One of the most important things district nurses do is to give advice to old people and their relatives on both chronic and acute illness. Often one or two visits from a nurse can solve a number of problems by answering your questions, and so relieving your anxieties. It is therefore as appropriate to contact the nurse when your elderly relative is acutely ill and confined to bed – with pneumonia, for example – as it is to seek her help in chronic illness.

You can contact the district nursing service by asking at the health centre or surgery. District nurses are not employed by the general practitioner, but each general practitioner usually has a small number of nurses working with her. Alternatively, you can contact the nursing service directly; look up 'Nurses' in the telephone directory.

There are also private nursing agencies in the *Yellow Pages*. These, however, are expensive – so do not employ a private nurse until you have asked the advice of the NHS district nursing service.

Practice nurse

Some health centres have a practice nurse who works in the health centre's treatment room. Her main contact with older people is in the treatment of leg ulcers.

The health visitor

The health visitor is a State Registered Nurse who has had special training in preventive medicine. She is therefore a very useful source of advice on matters such as diet and exercise. She has also been specially trained to help people to cope with the social consequences of disease, such as housing and income problems, and is therefore an appropriate person to ask about social security or housing benefits. It is not the health visitor's job to know all the complicated details of social security – neither is it her job to fill out forms, although she is usually willing to help people who find form-filling impossible – but she does know her way around the system, and can act as a guide to the maze of welfare benefits.

The health visitor can be contacted in the same way as the district nurse.

Hospital Services

Older people use every hospital service with the exception of paediatrics and obstetrics, but two are of particular importance: the psychogeriatric service (see p. 87) and geriatric medicine.

The department of geriatric medicine specializes in the problems of older people, and the services are offered by a team of professionals – the consultant in geriatric medicine, the occupational therapist and physiotherapist, the medical social worker and the specialist nurse. The range of services offered includes:

- domiciliary assessment – in the home of the old person
- out-patient assessment at a clinic
- day hospital care, both to provide treatments that cannot easily be given at home – for example, regular enemas – and to provide relief for carers when the person is too disabled to attend a social services day centre. Some people attend day hospital five days a week, but once a week may be sufficient to offer you relief and to allow staff to review progress and treatment
- emergency admissions in acute illness
- short-stay admissions to allow relatives to go on holiday: it is wise to ask for such an admission at least six months in advance
- regular short-stay admissions to give regular relief. The pattern varies to suit individual needs; it may be every weekend, or every second weekend, or one week in four, or whatever best meets the family's needs and can be fitted into the hospital's busy schedule
- long-stay care.

Referral to a department of geriatric medicine must be made by the old person's general practitioner.

How Can I Get More Help?

Some elderly people and their families can clearly define their requirements but are unable to obtain the help they need, and are told they will be put on a waiting list. Other old people and families are actually receiving help, but feel that they need more. In either case the problem is the same – how can I get more help?

There is no easy answer. The first fact to emphasize is that there is no point in becoming angry with the person who is helping you. You should certainly explain to the district nurse or home help why you think more help is essential, but the person who is actually helping can only do what she can in the hours available. Her time is divided between different old people after taking into account the needs of all of them, and when pressure of work is high – as it usually is – she has to discuss with her superior the fairest means of allocating her time among all those who need her help. There is equally little point in getting angry with the person who makes decisions about the allocation of help – for example, the consultant who has to decide that one old person should come to day hospital five days a week, and that another should come only two days a week. It is certainly important to explain to the person in charge why you think your need is such that you require more help than you are getting, but she can only try to be as fair as she can with the resources she has at her disposal, and if she gives *you* more help it is likely to be at the expense of someone else. If she has allocated less help to you than you feel is needed it is probably because she has had to allocate more help to some other family whose problem she judges to be greater. Almost certainly, the person in charge of the service will be pressing for more money so that she can give more help to everyone in need, but at any one time she can only try to be as fair as possible with the resources available to her.

If you feel that you are being treated unfairly and that you are not getting the help you need because the professionals do not appear to listen to you or like you, then you have a cause for complaint. If, as more usually happens, you feel that they are doing the best they can as fairly as they can, and the problem is simply a shortage of resources, you should write to the head of the whole service.

If you want to point out that a particular service needs more money in it, using your own problem as an example of the needs that are not being met, you should write to your local councillor, if it is a local authority service, or to the chairperson of the health authority if it is an NHS service. Your local community health council, which is listed in the telephone book, will also be interested to hear of shortfalls in the service.

If the reply you receive states that those who are responsible for the service are well aware of the shortage but can do no more because of government policy, you can write to your Member of Parliament. However, that should be the last person you approach, not the first.

If you write a letter about a shortage of services, remember to point out that you are not complaining about the help you are receiving – indeed you should praise your helpers if that is appropriate – but that it is the help you are not receiving which is the problem.

Should I Complain?

Services may cause dissatisfaction in a number of ways, but there are two common categories of problem – recurrent difficulties and isolated mistakes. Each needs a different approach.

Recurrent difficulties are those which you meet every time the old person receives a service. If, for example, the old person is always wet when she comes back from the day hospital, or if a care assistant always comes to put the old person to bed before she wants to go to bed, steps should be taken to try to improve the service. The first step is simply to inform those in charge about the problem, because they may not be aware of it. Older people are, in general, grateful for the help they get, and many do not like to point out the difficulties the services cause them, even if asked directly whether everything is satisfactory. Sometimes such difficulties can be easily solved once people know about them. In other cases it is less easy, but it is only very rarely that nothing can be done, and some compromise is usually possible. The best way of resolving this type of problem is by speaking directly to those involved.

When there has been a serious error – for example, the discharge of an old person from hospital without notice – a different approach is required. Nothing will undo the difficulties resulting from such a mistake and it is unlikely that a complaint will be of great benefit to the old person or to you, for such mistakes are usually isolated events in the life of any one old person, and rarely happen more than once to the same person. However, it is worth while asking for an explanation of the incident, because the investigation which your complaint will initiate may lead to an improvement in the efficiency of the service, and so reduce the risk that the same thing will happen to other people.

Each problem is different, and so is each complaint, but there are a few guidelines that are relevant in most cases:

- complain as soon after the incident as possible: the longer you wait, the more difficult the investigation
- put your complaint in writing: send it in the first instance to the person providing the service, and keep a copy of your letter
- ask for an interview if the letter of reply is unsatisfactory: it is easier to discuss the details of problems face to face than by letter
- if the professionals involved do not provide a satisfactory explanation you can write to your councillor if it is a local authority problem, or to the chairperson of your health authority if it is a problem with health services other than general practice, or the provision of dental, optical or pharmacy services. Complaints about these services should be made to the Family Practitioner Committee.

It may be necessary to write to your Member of Parliament or to the Ombudsman if the steps you have taken to obtain a satisfactory explanation from your local services are unsuccessful. The Citizens' Advice Bureau, or the Community Health Council, if it is a complaint about health services, will be able to advise you on how to do this most effectively.

Finally, remember that letters of complaint are relatively more common than letters of praise, and that those who have provided you with a good service will be greatly rewarded if you write to the top praising and commending the help they have given you.

Voluntary Organizations

Although modern society is often criticized for its attitude to the elderly, voluntary help is widespread and extremely important. It may be possible to arrange for a neighbour to keep an eye on your elderly relative, and go to see her only if her milk has not been taken in, or if her light does not go on in the evening: often neighbours do this without being asked. In addition to this type of informal support, a number of voluntary organizations exist. Their strength varies from place to place, and it is therefore necessary to find out which are most active in the area in which your elderly relative lives, by asking her health visitor or district nurse. Not all volunteers are keen on long-term commitments. Most prefer to perform tasks for a limited period of time: for example, most volunteers prefer the job of taking an old person to the optician a few times, rather than agreeing to take an old person to a day centre every week of the year.

Age Concern

There is an Age Concern office in every county and city, listed in the telephone directory. They are an excellent source of advice on all the problems of older people; they sell useful booklets and give out helpful leaflets. They are also a very good source of information on the voluntary services which are available in the area. They may also issue a 'consumer guide' to private old people's and nursing homes.

Citizens' Advice Bureau (CAB)

A good source of advice on legal, housing and social security problems, but they do not have the same specific expertise in the problems of older people as Age Concern.

Women's Royal Voluntary Service (WRVS)

Provides meals on wheels and organizes day centres and lunch clubs, but requests for meals on wheels are usually made to social services.

St John's, St Andrew's and Red Cross

These vary in strength from one place to another: in some places one is strong, in other places another. They provide useful courses in first aid and home nursing, and may organize lunch clubs, old people's clubs and visiting services. They may also be able to arrange transport for occasional visits to the surgery or dentist.

The church – 'Fish' and Good Neighbours schemes

The contribution of the church varies widely, but many churches now organize home visiting for the housebound, transport to church, day centres and lunch clubs. Some churches have also started 'Fish' schemes, which are really volunteer flying squads ready to tackle almost anything for a limited period. They might, for instance, care for an old person discharged without warning from hospital on a Friday afternoon, until home help can be arranged on the Monday. Sometimes the old person is given a card to put in the window if she is in difficulty, but most Fish schemes prefer to watch for less obvious signs of distress, such as the bottle of milk left on the doorstep. Good Neighbours schemes are similar to Fish schemes, but are not all based on a church.

Help the helpers

Remember that all voluntary organizations need both people and money. Give a donation if you have benefited from voluntary help or, even more important, give some of your own time and expertise.

CHAPTER 6

The Challenge of Mental Illness

The burden of caring for a physically disabled relative is often very heavy, but the challenge posed by old people who are mentally ill can be even greater, particularly if the old person is confused.

Confusion

A person who is confused has a poor memory. He may be able to remember where he was born and brought up, but be unable to remember who has been to see him the previous day, or even whether he has eaten his lunch or not. The loss of memory, which takes place normally as we age, does not interfere with our ability to live an independent life. We may have to use a shopping list where we relied on our memory before, and we may find it more difficult to remember names, but we will not be seriously inconvenienced. If a person's forgetfulness is causing difficulties in daily life, the general practitioner should be consulted.

Rapid onset

Confusion involves a loss of the ability to think logically – for example, not being capable of looking after money or of carrying on an intelligent conversation. Normal ageing does not result in serious intellectual impairment, and if you notice that your relative is not thinking clearly the general practitioner should be consulted, especially if the change has come on rapidly.

If confusion develops over the course of a few days, weeks or months, it is probably the result of a physical disease which is either reducing the amount of oxygen to the brain or increasing the concentration of toxic chemicals in the brain. Chest infections, urinary infections, heart failure, heart attacks: these and many other treatable illnesses can cause confusion, as can the side-effects of many drugs and medicines, including alcohol. Prompt referral is therefore important if you have noticed the rapid onset of confusion, because it may have a treatable cause.

Slow onset

Confusion may develop much more slowly, over many months or a few years. At first the problem is thought to be no more than normal ageing, but gradually the memory failure interferes with daily life. The door key is lost on a number of occasions, pans are left to boil dry and food goes mouldy in the cupboard. Medical assessment is also essential in confusion of slow onset, because it too may have a treatable cause, such as thyroid disease. However, in most cases the cause is dementia, and only a small proportion of cases of dementia are treatable.

The term 'dementia' simply means that there is death of brain tissue, and the most common sort of dementia is sometimes called 'senile dementia of Alzheimer's type' or, more usually, Alzheimer's Disease. The cause of Alzheimer's Disease is not known at present, and consequently neither treatment nor prevention are possible. The second most common type of dementia is that which results from narrowing of the arteries to the brain, with a decrease in the supply of oxygen to the brain, and the consequent death of brain cells. There are other less common types of dementia, some of which are treatable, so accurate diagnosis is always important. This is particularly the case with depression, since it can sometimes cause so much agitation that the old person may be thought to have dementia, when in fact he is depressed.

The course of Alzheimer's Disease varies from one person to another. Some people decline quickly, others less so. Although the rate of decline cannot be slowed by any medical treatment, there are aggravating factors which increase the rate of decline, and these can be influenced. The five major factors are shown in the table.

Aggravating factor	Possible preventive actions
Isolation	1 Increase number of visitors. 2 Increase number of trips out of home. 3 Provide a pet.
Sensory deprivation	1 Ask general practitioner to check hearing, if it appears to fail (see p. 43). 2 Have eyes checked regularly (see p. 41). 3 Encourage movement and activity.
Physical illness	Report sudden deterioration to general practitioner, as confusion of rapid onset can complicate dementia, particularly if the person is too confused to report any physical disease.
Side-effects of drugs	Try to prevent problems with drugs: people with dementia are particularly sensitive to certain drugs (see p.48).
Family tensions	1 Try to keep your own health and strength as good as possible. 2 Try not to bottle up your thoughts and feelings.

The need for a straightforward approach to the old person with dementia cannot be overemphasized. If he makes a mistake, correct it as you would correct someone who does not have dementia. If he does something odd – asks for breakfast in the middle of the afternoon, for example, point this out to him. Make sure the old person has a clock that works, and a calendar that is kept up to date.

How to organize the day

Although it may not seem to matter to a confused person whether it is day or night, a routine is in fact of great importance in helping the affected person to remain calm and happy. Regular times for waking, rising, meals and going to bed are all helpful, and the old person should be told the time as often as possible, for example: 'Come on, Dad, it's one o'clock, lunch time.'

The development of a regular rhythm will do much to prevent sleeping problems and broken nights. An early start to the day, some physical exercise (preferably outside) and a regular evening ritual are more effective than sleeping pills – and this is true whether or not an old person has dementia. The routine in the evening should follow the same pattern: a meal, some entertainment, perhaps television, a quiet time with no television, a hot drink. This pattern, kept to the same times each evening, will, with a warm bed, promote sleep. It is also useful to encourage the old person to empty the bladder last thing before retiring.

Exercise, both mental and physical, is important and a walk outside every day is very helpful, not only in keeping the old person fit but also in providing stimulation, promoting sleep and preventing 'wandering'. Relatives are understandably upset when an old person with dementia 'wanders', but the person who 'wanders' is simply someone who has either set off for somewhere but forgotten how to get there, or who has gone for a walk and forgotten how to get home.

Talking to a confused person

One of the most upsetting aspects of dementia is the impact which it has on the old person's ability to communicate with you. The person's attention wanders, she may make illogical remarks, she may not appear to hear or be influenced by what other people say, or she may repeat herself. These depressing characteristics are in part the consequences of dementia, but they may also be caused or aggravated by the way in which other people speak to the confused person, and there are some guidelines for good communication which can make conversation less upsetting for you, and less confusing for the old person.

- If you hold the old person's hand while talking you may engage his attention more effectively, at the same time as giving him the comfort and communication of physical contact.
- Minimize distracting background noise – switch off the television and radio.
- Give more information than you would to someone who does not have dementia; for example, by saying, 'I met Tom Johnson who used to work beside you,' rather than simply saying, 'Tom was asking for you.'
- Speak to the old person about his past, showing him photographs and, if possible, playing music he enjoyed in the past.
- Correct mistakes as they are made. But if an old person keeps making the same mistake – such as saying he is waiting for his mother who has been dead many years – try to distract his mind from this train of thought by walking with him to another room, or by making him something to eat, or by taking out a pack of cards and starting to play with him.

If you find talking to your elderly relative is becoming an experience which is frequently distressing, ask the general practitioner for advice. He may suggest referral to a psychologist or psychiatric community nurse as a means of helping to improve communication, or he may be able to suggest measures himself.

Behaviour problems

It is not only what a person with dementia says that is important, it is what he does – his behaviour. There are two types of behaviour problem, and each affects relatives and helpers in a different way.

The first is the problem that is obviously abnormal, for example, undressing and walking out of the house partly clothed, or refusal to eat or go to bed. This type of problem is not only a major source of worry; the impact on you and the family is also immediately obvious to professionals, friends and neighbours. Anti-social behaviour is not an inevitable complication of Alzheimer's Disease. Many old people who have dementia do not pose serious behaviour problems. Therefore, when you come across such a problem, you should seek help, either from the general practitioner or, if the old person is in contact with a psychiatric hospital, with one of the professionals working there who knows him (see p. 87). If the general practitioner's advice is not effective, the district nurse or health visitor can be approached, or you can go to the social services department (see p. 88) for advice. The suggestions that you will be given will usually be of ways in which you can prevent such problems, or change the upsetting behaviour when it occurs by altering your own reaction to it. Tranquillizers have a very limited part to play in treating this type of problem.

The second type of problem is one which is much less obvious to the person who is not directly affected. The upsetting behaviour in this case may simply be an unhygienic habit, such as the way the old person picks his nose, or some repetitive act, such as a nervous cough, or something that the old person keeps repeating. It is this type of behaviour which drives many relatives to distraction and to thoughts of violence – for it is very common to feel hostile thoughts or to consider hitting an elderly relative whose behaviour is consistently annoying or frustrating. Usually irritation with one such aspect of the old person's behaviour is a symptom of general feelings of annoyance and frustration, and these feelings are in turn often symptoms of the carer's fatigue and need for relief.

You may think that it is ridiculous to seek professional help for such an apparently small problem. However, if you find one aspect of the old person's behaviour continually annoying, or feel like hitting him, you should seek help in changing the old person's behaviour, or your own reaction to it, if the simple step of telling the old person to stop it has proved ineffective. The professional whom you consult may be able to suggest some way of modifying the annoying behaviour, or may simply arrange for you to have a relief to reduce your tiredness and increase your tolerance. Often it is helpful to tell someone that you have felt like hitting your elderly relative. If you do so you will *not* be reported to the police, or put in a special file, or marked out for close attention. This reaction is very common and understandable. It is good to have the courage to admit to it, because you may be relieved by sharing your thoughts and your guilty feelings with someone else, and because it gives the general practitioner or social worker an indication of the effects that the stress of caring is having on you.

Incontinence Owing to Mental Illness

When incontinence comes from dementia or a stroke, the problem is not the result of disease affecting the lower bowel or the bladder. It results from loss of control of bowel and bladder, and a different approach is therefore necessary.

Prevention of faecal incontinence

The following steps can be helpful:

1. Prevent constipation by increasing the amount of fibre in the old person's diet (see p. 27). Ask the general practitioner, district nurse or health visitor if you are uncertain how best to do this.
2. Do not give laxatives, and try to dissuade the old person from using them.
3. Encourage the old person to try to have a bowel motion at a regular time every day. If he formerly had a regular pattern, for example 'going after breakfast', maintain this; if not, pick a time that is convenient for you to remind him.
4. Seek the advice of the general practitioner or district nurse if the old person becomes constipated or if you notice soiling. Smears of faeces on sheets or underwear are one sign of constipation, and an enema may be necessary if a person has become seriously constipated.

If faecal incontinence develops, the district nurse is the best source of advice on how to cope with the problem.

Prevention of urinary incontinence

The following measures can be helpful.

1. Encourage the old person to pass water regularly, for example every two hours during the day.

2. Ensure that the old person is still able to manage his or her clothing when at the toilet: ask the district nurse for advice if difficulty with dressing or undressing is causing 'accidents' in the toilet.
3. Do not allow the old person to drink pints of fluid before going to bed, but do not dehydrate him either: offer, for example, a cup of tea at six and a cup of cocoa at nine.
4. Ensure that it is easy for the old person to pass water at night (see p. 34).

If the old person develops urinary incontinence, ask the advice of the district nurse. She may suggest that the old person wears special underwear which can hold absorbent pads, or the use of special sheets which will help to keep the old person's skin healthy. A catheter may be the best way of keeping the person dry, but permanent catheters have their problems, so the decision to insert one is not taken until all other measures have failed.

When incontinence becomes worse

If the incontinence suddenly becomes more difficult to cope with – if, for example, the old person is not only unable to reach the toilet, but goes to urinate in some completely inappropriate place such as the corner of the lounge, ask the general practitioner for advice. Deterioration like this is a symptom of some other problem, which may be physical or emotional.

The Psychogeriatric Service

In every health authority there is a psychogeriatric service for elderly people with mental illness. The service is staffed by a psychiatrist (sometimes called a psychogeriatrician) and psychiatric nurses, and there will often be a social worker, occupational therapist and psychologist, working as members of the team. The service usually provides:

- assessment in the old person's home
- day hospitals to relieve relatives or to start new forms of treatment
- short-term admissions for assessment and treatment
- short-term admissions to allow relatives to go on holiday – ask six months in advance if you need a break
- regular short-term admissions to provide regular periods of relief
- long-stay care.

Social services also give home help day care, short-term admissions and long-stay care in old people's homes for people with mild degrees of dementia, and you can approach the social services department for help directly. Access to the psychogeriatric service, which helps more severely affected people, is by the general practitioner's referral only.

The prevention of exhaustion in people caring for someone with dementia is now a high priority for both health and social services, and the provision of relief from caring is an effective method. Seek help early when you feel the strain increasing and the stress rising.

Depression

Depression is normal. Everyone becomes depressed from time to time. To help overcome an old person's depression:

- try to arrange more visitors if he is isolated
- take him out of the house for a visit to a friend or a trip
- encourage him to think of someone who makes him feel happy

– a grandson or daughter, for example. Provide photographs of this person, and even a tape recording to supplement any visits that person can make.

You should encourage the old person to seek help from his general practitioner if any of the following features develop and last for more than a couple of days:

- loss of appetite
- loss of wish to go out
- disregard for personal appearance
- agitation and restlessness associated with the depression
- depression breaking in on his thoughts when he is speaking to you.

If the old person speaks of suicide or says that he is 'thinking of doing away with himself', or gives any indication that he might do so, you should seek help promptly yourself, even if the old person is unwilling to consult his general practitioner. Treatment of depression with drugs is often effective when the depression is severe, but hospital treatment may be necessary if the drugs prescribed by the general practitioner do not relieve it.

Anxiety

Anxiety, like depression, is a normal experience. It can usually be reduced by dealing with its cause or by reducing the old person's isolation. If, however, anxiety persists and is seriously affecting the quality of the old person's life – for example, her ability to sleep or enjoy the company of her grandchildren – the advice of the general practitioner should be sought. He may prescribe tranquillizers, but in many cases the reassurance of someone who is known and trusted by the old person will reduce the levels of anxiety to a more tolerable level.

CHAPTER 7

Coping with Confused Behaviour in the Family

If you live with your mother or father and therefore see him or her on a daily basis, it will be less likely that you will be as critical of changes in behaviour as someone who sees him or her only once in a while. In most cases mental confusion comes in the form of different symptoms, and it comes on slowly. There are recognizable signs; the old person may:

- become forgetful
- be confused about money
- begin to hide money and say that you or a neighbour has taken it
- lose balance
- become aggressive
- be unable to attend to simple tasks such as dressing and undressing.

Your first reaction to these problems will probably be to decide that they are just part of getting old. Or, although you may realize that something is seriously wrong, you may refuse to admit to yourself or to anyone else what is really happening, because you are ashamed. The stigma of 'mental illness in the family' still lingers, and you could feel that people will be unkind and talk about your parent's changed behaviour in offensive terms. That can be hurtful.

You will be reacting as most other people do in your position, if, the first time she doesn't know you, you say anxiously, 'This is me, I'm your daughter, remember!' You may even cry, and you may have a terrible sense of loss. A woman we know rang home and her father didn't recognize either her voice or her name; she said she absolutely panicked.

If your parent lives alone and you see changes in progress, you will have to decide what to do. Answers to the following questions should be a useful guide.

- Is she managing to eat regularly and take any prescribed medicines?
- Is she wandering and at risk?
- Does she leave pots and pans on the stove?
- Is she becoming too troublesome to the neighbours?

For a while meals on wheels, disconnecting the stove and so on, may help. Moving house will probably make her condition worse. Talk to her about any changes you think have to be made. Generally she will say she is all right, and she may fight the suggestion of leaving her home.

If you intend to bring her to live with you, talk to your family first. Ask yourself whether your parent and the family will each have a degree of privacy. It may be that a residential home or hospital is the answer.

When your parent is living with you and her condition gets worse, you will find it increasingly difficult to cope. Some of the changes you can expect are:

- her whole attitude to you may well be transformed for the worse, and your once gentle, loving parent may become demanding and unpleasant
- she may even be abusive; some formerly dear old ladies and old gentlemen begin to swear like troopers
- she may even tell you, 'You're a thief, the neighbour's a

prostitute and the minister's a crook.' It is all part of some disease of the brain, and increasingly she will not recognize you

- she may decide that you are her long dead mother or her sister
- she may talk on and on about her childhood, about people you never knew, or repeat the same questions over and over.

If you are there with her alone all week you can begin to wonder about your own sanity.

How to Help

It will be much better if, as soon as you recognize what is really happening, you talk to your mother's doctor. Get a medical assessment, because the condition may be due to an infection, to thyroid gland problems, to a vitamin deficiency, or to depression from the side-effects of drugs. The doctor will be able to make the proper diagnosis. Write down any changes as you notice them, because it is very easy to forget some things when you get to the doctor. Ask him to explain the condition fully and tell you what to expect.

It will not be easy for you to accept that she has a type of mental confusion. But you will cope better if you can come to terms with the diagnosis. It will be easier for you to care for her if you understand what is happening.

Accept that the changes in her behaviour are symptoms of an illness. Sadly, the sufferer does have fleeting moments of being normal and must be terribly hurt and distressed by an apparent lack of understanding. Imagine how you yourself would feel if your child became impatient with you. Remember, she will not appreciate the reason for your impatience. In the beginning she will get upset and try to pretend that her mind is not going. You can be helpful and make things as easy as you can. For instance, when you get up, tell her what day it is, remind her that it is the day she goes to the day centre, and so on. Provide as many memory joggers as you can think of. These hints will help her:

- get a large calendar – the travel agency ones generally have large print
- leave a note of the names of other members of the family around
- a picture of the loo on the door can remind her that the door opens into the loo
- if you have to go out, leave a clearly written message of where you are. Be reassuring before you go so that she will not be agitated while you are away.

Safety

If you look at what is worrying you most, you will probably put safety at the top of the list. These are steps you can take to protect her and her property from accidents:

- make sure stairs and passages are well lit and obstacle-free
- put hand-rails on the stairs to give her more support
- if you have an open fire, put a sturdy fireguard in front of it. You ought to consider an alternative heating system such as a convector fire. This will make her safer and relieve your anxiety
- an electric cooker is safer than a gas cooker
- try to keep her away from the kitchen while you are cooking. Put pans filled with cold water on the rings of a cooling electric cooker, to protect her from accidentally touching them.

If she can still get to the loo and also bath herself, make sure that it is all as easy as possible. The occupational therapist will advise on bathroom aids and adaptations:

- there are frames that can be placed around the loo and high loo seats
- you might provide a bath seat and non-slip mats
- check that there are no cord flexes trailing, or shabby lino or carpet ends about

Eating

The appetites of dementia patients can vary from time to time. Sometimes you just cannot tempt them, and at other times they will finish a substantial meal and then announce that they have not eaten for ages. The best way to deal with eating problems is to prepare small meals frequently. You can help her by serving her food in bits which are easy to manage with fork or spoon.

In cases where the old person will only nibble and is missing out on her proper nourishment, put a mixture of wholesome foods into the liquidizer. For instance, an egg, milk, a tablespoon of wheatgerm and a banana whisked up in a food processor or liquidizer and topped with grated nutmeg can be very tempting – easy to drink down as well as tasty.

Ask the health visitor (see p. 71) if you get worried that she is not getting adequate vitamins. If she picks at her food and eats slowly, buy a food warmer and an insulated cup to keep the meal more appetizing. Sew towelling over plastic backing to make a large cover-up napkin to stop clothes from getting messy. You can tuck it into the neck. Do not use a baby bib unless you really have to, because that can be hurtful and make her feel worse at the times when she is normal.

Medicine

Giving medication can be difficult, and pills can be spat back over and over. Ask her doctor to prescribe in liquid form whenever possible.

If she is forgetful, do not leave her medication doses up to her, because she may over-dose or under-dose. If you have to leave her to take the medicine alone, never leave more than the day's supply. Lock away the rest of it.

Health and appearance

Many patients refuse to bath or to clean their teeth, and it can prove exhausting to keep them generally clean; although we all like privacy to bath, you may have to insist you will help:

- always run the cold water into the bath first
- do not fill the bath too full
- make sure she has enough support to get in and out
- keep her hair washed and make sure her teeth and gums are kept clean.

Some old people develop odd habits, and dealing with fetishes can be tiring. Many old people stuff belongings into plastic bags and then carry them around.

It makes life easier for you if you have as little as possible in her wardrobe and dressing table. Do not be hurtful and remove everything. Leave several changes of clothing, and say you have stored the other things to keep the moths and silverfish out. Dressing can be a problem – if she has difficulty dressing:

- try laying out the clothes in the order of putting them on
- Do not fuss unduly if she puts a dress on back to front. The main thing is for her to be dressed and able to get about easily.

- Buy her easy-to-zip or fasten garments. Velcro is a great help (see p. 109).

Care of the face is as important to old people's dignity as to everyone else. Some old ladies have quite a growth of hair on the face; while they are able to take care of themselves, they keep it shaven and so preserve their feminine appearance. When they can no longer cope, someone else must shave them to prevent unnecessary distress.

Do not neglect her need for exercise and diversion just because she is confused; you will need to provide a lot of support and help in this area. Because of her condition she may need encouragement to keep busy at some craft or hobby or to join in group activities. She may get restless and start and stop, but gently coax her.

A dear old man we knew rode his horse every day until the very end. He loved the horse and he was somewhat at risk, but his whole day revolved around feeding, watering, grooming, harnessing and riding his horse. Because of his illness he could not remember much else, and he died a week after he gave up going to see the horse. Many old people relate well to animals, and animals seem to understand them. An old dog can be very long-suffering, loyal and companionable.

Quite a few old people love small children, and find them very reassuring, too. Photos of members of the family on the wall around the bed can also be very comforting.

As most old people sit down a lot, make sure that her chair is comfortable. Parker Knoll and Cintique make armchairs with higher seats which are easier to get out of. See that the seat is firm.

If there is a television in the room, check that it cannot easily be knocked off the stand and collapse on her feet or shins.

Friends and the family

Keeping up contacts for as long as possible will help both her and you. If she enjoys ringing up her friends and family, encourage her, even though she may talk endless nonsense. You can get a special handset from the local telephone office if she is hard of hearing.

Some demented old people still show an interest in sex and are comforted by their partner cuddling them; only the partners can decide whether to keep up this side of life. Some old men mistake their daughters for their deceased wives, and make sexual advances. Try not to over-react – recognize it as part of the illness. Sometimes patients admitted to hospital end up in somebody else's bed, and the staff will quietly and gently take them back to their own beds.

Do not shut old people out – talk to them. Remember that you will feel simply awful later on for having lost your patience.

Even though you may be embarrassed about things she says or does, persevere in taking her out. She may insult the waiters at the café, but you take them aside and explain; or she may say the food at a friend's house has been poisoned, but if they are understanding and pass it off, it will mean that both of you get a change of scene.

However much you feel a change away will do her good, understand that the unfamiliar holiday place, and getting to and from it, can cause upset and make her permanently worse.

Do not decide that because she is mentally confused or depressed she cannot do or enjoy anything. The old man who loved his horse found little in life he enjoyed but the horse. It would have been easy for his wife to decide he was at risk or ought not to go up to the field, but she let him keep going. It gave her some breathing space and helped her to keep going, too.

Be tactfully helpful if the old person is struggling to do

something, but try not to take over. Letting them feel useful and part of the household will help them and give them a continuing sense of security. There will be occasions when you have got to make a decision to exclude them, such as when there are lots of strangers in the house. They will be bound to get upset and disoriented. Gently explain that it is not really her scene and distract her with the suggestion she watch the television, or invite her to have a chat or go for a walk.

Other problems to watch for

It is important not to concentrate solely on mental aspects. Perhaps your parent is having difficulty reading or sewing, or she may have arthritis setting in. Any physical condition will make her feel a lot worse, and not make caring any easier for you. For instance she may fidget and wander off when you put her in front of the television while you get on with some chores. The real cause of her wandering off may not be her confusion, but the fact that she cannot hear or see properly. So do not put all behaviour down to the one cause.

Some of the problems a carer will have to deal with will be new to her, and prove not only physically but emotionally exhausting.

One of the symptoms of dementia is restlessness. Some old people who suffer from dementia do not seem to need much sleep. They think they hear knocking at the door, or decide they have to go somewhere. They get mixed up about day and night. Their illusions will disturb you and you will not get your proper rest.

- You may have to ask her doctor to prescribe some medication to help her to sleep.
- A night light left on can be reassuring to her.

- Try to keep her on the move during the day so that she gets tired out.
- If you do have to get up, be gentle – remember she got up God knows how many times when you were a small child.
- Check that her room has fresh air, but that on the other hand it is not too cool.
- Cold feet can keep anyone awake. If she suffers from them, buy or knit her bedsocks.

Wandering is one of the main causes of anxiety when you are caring for the elderly confused. A confused person will often go off clad in only a nightdress in the middle of winter. She may walk for miles before getting exhausted. If your parent is prone to wandering off, get an identity bracelet for her so that whoever comes across her will know she belongs at your address. Have complicated locks put on doors and gates. Often, if she is deterred she will give up trying to get out into the street.

One of the most tiring changes in behaviour which you may find is where the old person follows the carer from room to room. This can put the carer under a lot of pressure, because you will feel you do not have a minute to yourself. Probably the only way you will cope with this is by getting friends or neighbours to come in and take over while you have a bath, or just sit in your room or in the garden, or get right away from the house.

Some dementia sufferers imagine all manner of strange things. They can think an old friend is in the room or that they can hear people whispering next door. Try to go along with the idea and say something such as, 'I can't hear them or see them', or try to distract her with a cup of tea or by putting the television on, or by putting the cat on her lap.

One of the most difficult effects of dementia is the accusation stage. It is not unknown for old people to tell people they are being pinched, half-starved, and struck. Relatives will feel mortified. Generally there is no truth in most claims. Professionals follow up cases where they suspect the old person is being abused.

Dealing with aggression, and sometimes even violence, can be distressing. It is not only the fact that someone you knew as docile is now violent and throws things or lunges out which is upsetting, but it is hard to accept that this person is your parent, to whom you looked up and who went to bat for you when you needed it. Quite often such behaviour is sparked off by your being very firm, saying something such as 'Stop that', or 'It is bath time.' It may take all your will-power not to retaliate. Calmly try to remember that the behaviour is not in fact aimed at you. You may even have to count up to ten, or go out of the room for a moment. If you feel fed up, do not sit and smoulder, call the doctor in, or a friend, and let off steam or say 'Look, it's time somebody took over, I just have to get away from it.'

Incontinence

Often the dementing person becomes incontinent: see Chapter 3 for advice on this common problem.

If the incontinence gets to the stage where she needs pads and pants, ask the district nurse to provide them. When she uses them, make sure she does not suffer chafing – the chafing can be very uncomfortable and cause her to be distressed. At the stage of constant bed changing, inquire whether or not there is a laundry service for incontinent persons' linen.

She may be too confused to keep track of her visits to the toilet – she may become constipated and you may not know about it. Try to check that she is going regularly – otherwise she may need an enema (see p. 23). Watch the amount of roughage in her diet just as she watched your diet when you were dependent on her.

Double incontinence can cause grave distress to the dependant and the carer. The odour and sometimes anti-social behaviour of spreading faeces over walls and clothing can be distressing to watch and to clean up. Being able to cope with changed behaviour involves understanding that the person does not know what is going on, most or all of the time, and that his or her actions are not deliberately meant to anger and hurt you. Knowing this will make it easier for you to put up with what is happening. Your attitude is all-important. You will only manage if you are able to admit when you need help and can no longer cope alone.

Do not set down any hard and fast rules. Try to be flexible within a structure, so that your routine is open to change when necessary.

Looking After Yourself

Some relatives do get impatient. Carers who lose control are generally those who have other problems, or who are absolutely worn down. Carers who are inadequate persons at any time may push or shove, shout at or strike an old person. It is a criminal offence to assault and batter anyone, and carers will be well advised to bear in mind the consequences of such behaviour. If you feel exhausted and are at your wit's end, do not carry on without seeking out advice and help.

Obviously if your dependant has some form of dementia, you are going to have to get some respite to keep your own health. Shop around for statutory or voluntary sitters-in. Inquire about day care facilities. The social worker can advise you. There are some day centres which particularly cater to taking mentally confused patients for a day. Ask the old person's general practitioner about short-term admissions.

When you have your periodic rests (for a week or two) it is better to make arrangements for someone to come in to look after her.

Plan the substitute carer's takeover carefully. Ask her to come and introduce herself, then get her to come for an hour or so before you actually leave. The old person will be more likely to settle down with her if she feels she knows her. When she comes, explain your parent's condition, how you cope, her likes and dislikes. Encourage the substitute to be companionable, in such ways as playing cards or draughts with her so that she will not feel left out and lonely.

Some substitute carers will come for a small fee and travelling expenses. Inquire at voluntary organizations such as Age Concern or the National Council for Carers and their Elderly Dependants. Or, if money is no object, you should pay for a private nurse. BUPA Nursing Services is a useful contact source (36 Dover Street, London WI Tel: 01-629 4233).

Grief and guilt

It is quite normal for you to feel something close to grief about her condition. You will be sad that the person you have known all your life has changed out of all recognition. You may be relieved, and have a great sense of freedom if she goes to hospital, but then, too, you may start to miss her. We are selfish in wanting to cling to our loved ones whatever their condition, but this is only natural. You may even try to convince yourself that she will recover, and then feel let down that she does not.

Guilt is not a pleasant emotion, and caring can produce some guilty feelings. You may feel guilty about your impatience. You can wish she would die so you would not have to cope any longer, and later experience awful guilt at the thought.

If the disease gets worse, you may recognize that the time has come when you just cannot manage any longer. Perhaps she does not even recognize you. Your own health, your age, your patience level, how tired you are, the availability of statutory and voluntary back-up and how much you can afford to pay, are all important in determining when and whether you seek expert help. A geriatric or psychiatric hospital may be the answer. Do not make any decisions until you have taken professional advice and talked to other members of your family, or to friends; they will be better placed to be objective.

Do not feel guilty, or that you have let her down, as you really had no alternative. It will be a sad time for you and you will need friends and family to give you emotional support.

If your parent is mentally confused then you may need advice from the Court of Protection (see pp. 158–9).

For further information on dementia, we recommend *Caring for the Person with Dementia*, published by the Alzheimer's Disease Society (see p. 160).

CHAPTER 8

Some Practicalities of Caring and Nursing at Home

A basic knowledge of home nursing will help you and help your dependant. Remember that she probably finds it just as difficult to be dependent on you as you find it to be at her beck and call. Adjusting to illness is never easy. A happy attitude will help you both. If highly skilled nursing is needed, her general practitioner will arrange for the district nurse to come in. Find out as much as possible about her condition, so that you will have a better-informed approach to her care. Go to a home nursing course if you can. When you are nursing her make sure you know under what circumstances to call the doctor. Try to be sensible and do not call her if you can really cope. On the other hand, do not be foolhardy and try to cope beyond your experience and information. Know the danger signals.

Living Arrangements

The basis of good caring is planning. The room where she is to spend most of her time should be as big, bright and beautiful as possible. A lonely sick old person cannot help feeling a burden if she is bundled into a dingy dull worn-out room.

Warmth and good ventilation are essential. If you cannot afford professional double-glazing, cling-film over the windows is a cheap, clean and easy way to exclude window draughts. Buy a roll, which is usually 30 cm (approximately 12 in.) in width. Make sure that the painted or wooden surface is clean. Gently unwind one or two inches of the film; support the roll by inserting your two little fingers into the ends of the tube. Grasp the corners of the unrolled film between your first fingers and thumbs and offer up the film to the surface of the window frame with the mounting from the far side of the roll. Press the film against the front and use your thumbs to knead out any air bubbles caught between the film and the paintwork. Holding the roll steady with one hand, extend the grip of the film on the paintwork by gently stroking and kneading the film with the fingers of the other hand. When you have a good grip with the paintwork across the entire width of the film, allow the roll to unfold gently and lay the film under slight tension over the window frame. Carefully remove the roll by cutting the film against the paintwork with a razor blade. To remove crinkles, start in one of the top corners. Pick off the film and break the seal over a short distance, stretch the film slightly and seal back on to the paintwork. Repeat this process all the way around the edge of the film and you will remove all wrinkles.

The place where the old person will spend all or most of her time should be as organized and comfortable as possible. Make sure that there is enough cupboard space for storing nursing equipment. Here are some points to note.

- A single bed which is firm is ideal. (A husband and wife should stay together as long as they can in their bed.)
- For the old person who can not or will not go as far as the bathroom, put a chair commode in one corner and pull it close to the bed when she needs it.
- It is essential to have a bedside table with a lamp and enough space for whatever the old person might want.

- If she can get up, make sure that there is a comfortable armchair with a high seat.
- Carpeting prevents skids and tripping.
- Drawstring drapes keep out the light at night.
- If you have a choice, use a room which is big enough not to look cramped and which is easy to clean.
- A coat of paint will bring freshness to the room.
- A painting or wall-hanging breaks the monotony of four walls.
- Put her paraphernalia around – they will be the things from which she derives comfort and which bring back memories.

Whenever it can be arranged, allow the person to look out on to a garden or pleasant view. Her own television and radio will give her some independence. Provide her with remote controls where they are available, so she can choose her own programmes easily from a chair or bed.

Food

Diet is important. Before making any significant changes in anybody's type or quantity of food intake, check with the doctor. Regular eating habits, balance and appearance of food are good digestive aids; aroma, taste and flavour do stimulate the proper secretion of digestive juices, which change the food we eat into body-building materials.

Hot food left to get cold can be very unappetizing. This can be avoided by using a hot-plate available from most department stores, but food should not be kept hot for long periods of time and care should be taken with reheated food.

Do not spoon-feed unless you really have to, because it robs an old person of that side of her independence. There are easy-to-handle cups and eating tongs available. Be sure never to try to spoon-feed when a patient is lying down, as she may well choke.

Do not neglect your own eating habits. Remember that a well-balanced meal taken in relaxed circumstances is vital for your own mental and physical well-being. Be firm (when her needs are not urgent, of course) and insist on setting aside periods for your own meals.

Mobility

Getting about, however slowly or poorly, is important to the old person's independence and attitude as well as to the carer's workload. There is a walking stick, a zimmer frame, a tripod and a stair lift to give support. Ask the occupational therapist, or write to the Disabled Living Foundation for their catalogue (see p. 162). Below are some suggestions for you; check with a professional.

If you have to help her up narrow stairs, get behind her and support her by putting one hand under each of her armpits. Encourage her to grip the stair railing step by step.

If she has had a stroke and is trying to get about again, you can support her by placing yourself so you are beside her and slightly turned towards her, and

- putting one arm around her waist from behind, and the other under her armpit from in front, then blocking her feet with your forward foot, and
- arranging your body so your knee will support her weaker side when she steps forward, get her to walk.

The rhythm is: stick in front, bad leg forward, then strong leg forward – over and over.

If you have to help someone quite helpless out of a chair:

- stand just to one side of the chair and put one foot in front of hers to stop her edging forwards
- make sure that the chair cannot move

- bend your legs at the knees and put your hands under her armpits, then
- keeping your back straight, straighten your legs and help her into a standing position.

Make sure she is quite balanced before you move your feet and allow her to walk. Be ready to help if need be.

If you think your dependant needs a wheelchair, contact his or her doctor or hospital consultant to complete an application form. An occupational therapist may talk to the person about what type of wheelchair suits the patient, or ask whether the British Red Cross can supply one.

Knowing how to help someone into a car is useful:

- open the car door and put down the window; hold the door open
- protect her head with one hand
- steady her, and get her to grasp the car door where the door and window space meet, then twist around to sit backwards on to the seat
- lift her feet in if necessary.

To help her out of the car, do the opposite.

Practical aids

It is kind to encourage your dependant to do as much for herself as she can manage. It may take more time and try your patience, but it is something that will give her a sense of independence and help her to keep her dignity. If she has to re-learn the art, it will also give her a sense of achievement as she masters each movement again. The following will help her to dress.

A dressing stick can be made from an old wooden coat hanger. A V-notch cut out in the top side at one end will pull straps over the shoulder, a rubber thimble on the other end will cling to the clothing while the strap is being adjusted. A stocking aid helps to pull up the stockings; lazy tongs or an 'extend-a-hand' will perform the same function; a long-handled shoe horn helps people who cannot bend down to their feet. Selecting clothing which is easy to handle is important: slip-on shoes fastened with Velcro, a wrap-over skirt, a bra fastening at the front, a tie that fastens to the shirt with Velcro.

If you have to help her to dress, know some of the simple movements that will make the job easier for you and less undignified for her. If her arm is paralysed, slip your hand through the sleeve of the garment and hold her hand, then gently ease the sleeve along her arm. If you are putting on trousers, with the old person lying on the bed slip the trouser legs over and along first one leg and then the other leg. Pull them up as far as possible and help him to lift his buttocks off the bed, and then ease the trousers up to the waist and fasten them, or let him fasten them.

Sometimes old people need special clothes. Clothes adapted to her needs will help her and you. If she is mentally confused, clothes that are easy to put on and take off, without difficult fastenings, will cause her less frustration.

An arthritic sufferer will appreciate clothes that are easy to handle and fasten. Velcro fastenings are a help, as are slip-on shoes, wrap-on suits, special braces, tights instead of stockings (cut the gusset out to stop infections), ties with a Velcro grip. You can get french knickers and wrap-over-back style skirts for women; Velcro fastenings and special braces for men. The district nurse, the social worker, the occupational therapist or the Citizens' Advice Bureau can tell you where to get the above clothes. Fashionable clothes for the disabled can be bought from:

Dri Rider Ltd,
The Yews,
Highbridge,
Somerset TA9 4OE

Artimaze Ltd,
118 Wood Lane,
London NW9 7LX

Under the Chronically Sick and Disabled Persons Act 1970, the local authority social services department is required to provide aids to daily living for disabled persons living in their own homes. The following aids are among those available: bath aids, chairs, toilet seats, cutlery, kitchen aids, aids to dressing, handrails. Note that aids provided by social services may be subject to a charge at the discretion of the individual authority, and are considered to be on long-term loan.

Health authorities may supply the following: special beds, commodes, hoists for bed or bath, urinals, incontinence gear.

Apply for any such aids through the social worker, occupational therapist, health visitor, community nurse or doctor.

Bathing

If your parent is bed-bound or seriously ill and you are looking after her at home, you may feel that you cannot manage to bath her yourself. In this case, ask the general practitioner to send in the district nurse, or else contact her directly at the health centre. Where you think you ought to be able to cope, the following simple guidelines for a bedbath will give you more confidence.

- Have everything you need ready at hand – towels, face cloth, soap, powder, oil, nail file, nail scissors, toothbrush, toothpaste, tumbler of water, hair brush and comb, hand mirror, make-up or shaving gear when used, a change of clothes, extra blanket, bowl or container of water.
- Make sure that the bedroom is warm and draught-free.
- Fold back the bedclothes and cover your patient with the extra blanket.
- Pull the blanket back far enough to be able to help her get off her nightdress or pyjamas.

- Wash her face, neck and ears. Dry, dust on talcum powder.
- Wash and dry one arm at a time from her armpits to her fingers. Dust powder under her arms.
- Encourage her to wash her hands in the bowl of water.
- Wash and dry her front. Roll her on her side and wash her back. Check for pressure sore areas.
- Wash and dry each leg in turn. Wash each foot. If she is up to it, rinse the foot off in the bowl by bending her knee and letting her foot stand in the water.
- If she can, let her wash her genitals and bottom, or else do it for her.
- Do not let her get cold.
- Dress her in the fresh clothes.
- Help her to clean her teeth, clean her nails, cut her toenails and spray on some toilet water (keep it away from her eyes and nose).
- Brush her hair.
- Help her with make-up if she uses it. If it's a man help him to shave and rinse his face again.
- Finally, remake the bed with fresh linen.

If the old person can get to the bathroom and into the bath, these preparations will help.

- See that the bathroom is warm and has no draughts.
- Make sure all she needs is handy – soap, face cloth, towels, powder and clean clothes.
- Turn the cold water on first, and then add the hot and whisk the water around so the temperature is even.
- If she is unsteady on her feet, get a non-slip mat for the bath, a bath seat, rails on the bath or wall and special handles on the taps. (Ask the occupational therapist which equipment is the best.)
- If you have to help her into the bath, stand behind her and get

her to hold one wrist tightly with her other hand. Put your hands in between her body and her arms, and grasp her forearms in front of her waist.

- The next step is to let her step into the bath. You keep your back upright and bend your knees and lower her in on to the bath bottom or bath seat. Stay within earshot.
- If she cannot dry herself easily, get a roller towel put in.

Daily care of teeth, tongue, mouth and hair

It is essential to see that the old person's teeth, tongue and mouth are kept clean. If she is getting forgetful, she may neglect to remove her dentures.

Apart from the hygienic aspect of keeping a fresh dental plate, she herself will be more comfortable with one. See that any plate is put overnight into a glass of water containing denture cleaning powder. If she has her own teeth, make sure she has a periodic check-up (see p. 25). Remember that gum disease can be as destructive as tooth decay and that both can be attended to. (See Age Concern's excellent pamphlet on dental care.)

In cases where malodorous fur covers the teeth, or where the gums become painful, ask the district nurse what solutions to mix up to deal with the condition.

A woman never fails to be proud of her hair. A hair-do can lift flagging spirits and refresh dignity. When you can afford a hairdresser (and note that there are salons in lots of areas where a pensioner can get a reduced price hair-do), get one to wash and set your dependant's hair, and have your own hair done. One of the first indications of 'letting yourself go' is to allow your hair to become unkempt.

Preventing pressure sores

One of the most disturbing conditions for a bedridden patient is to have bed-sores, and you should take every measure to prevent them from developing.

- First of all, make sure she gets enough protein and Vitamin C. (Check with her doctor that these can be given.)
- If she is in bed during the day, change her position regularly, roughly every two hours. Discuss this with the general practitioner, and ask him about moving her at night.
- Make sure that the skin over the areas most likely to be affected is left clean and dry.
- Check that there are no crumbs or other bits and pieces on the bottom sheet, and keep it completely crease-free.
- Do not pull the patient up in the bed, lift her.
- Pillows can be used to relieve pressure on certain areas.
- A sorbo ring or water cushion relieves pressure on the buttocks.
- If the skin gets red or painful or tender, ask the advice of the district nurse. She may advise, or provide, a ripple bed.

In the event that pressure sores do develop, they must be treated with the same care as a wound. Always ask the advice of the general practitioner and the district nurse if a sore develops.

A sorbo ring to relieve pressure, sheepskin heel and elbow pads, rubber pillows or a bed-rest can do a great deal for her comfort. There are also various types of bed-rest. Ask the district nurse what she recommends. A triangular pillow adds comfort – a padded backrest with arms can be marvellous. If she is incontinent, incontinence aids (see p. 34) are a must.

Incontinence aids

Choosing helpful aids and equipment is important, and the old person's needs should be your guide. Perhaps constant reminders to go to the loo will mean that she can keep enough control not to wear incontinence pads and pants. Her mental and physical condition will have to be considered in any choice of aids you make; the devices described here can be very helpful.

Urinals for men are invaluable during the night, especially if an old man becomes very disorientated at night or is bed-bound. There are female urinals which require little moving of the old person, so that she may not have to be wide awake.

Incontinence pants are fitted and made of soft material with a waterproof pouch on the outside. The urine passes through the pants and is absorbed by a pad placed in the pouch. The skin stays dry.

A Kylie bed-sheet is a drawsheet with an underpad in one. The central part is made of soft, absorbent yellow quilted material. The urine spreads across the sheet's centre. The pad may be left under a patient for as long as twelve hours – what is particularly good about it is that the incontinent person is not lying in a pond all night, and the sheet can be laundered.

To dispose of soiled material, keep a plastic lined container handy. When the used pads are dropped in, the bag should be sealed and put out of the room.

In very severe cases the doctor may provide a catheter. The urine will drain into a bag which is either strapped to the leg or else supported by a waist belt. The bag is periodically emptied. The doctor or nurse will change the catheter to prevent the problem of infection.

The health authority refuse disposal service should collect soiled incontinence pads, dressings and other nursing waste which cannot be got rid of normally by persons caring for the sick person at home. Look in the telephone book under the district health authority's number, and ring and ask them to arrange this.

Easily adjustable clothing will cut down your workload and help the dignity of the old person. Wrap-over backs and French knickers are easier to manage than fussy dresses and ordinary underclothes. Nightdresses, dressing gowns and dresses are available with wrap-over backs in easily laundered materials. You do not have to buy new specially designed garments. It is easy enough to alter existing clothes. Long zips or Velcro fastenings can be added; dresses can be opened right down the front. The Women's Royal Voluntary Service have a booklet on alterations. The district nurse, social worker or Citizens' Advice Bureau will be able to tell you where special clothing can be bought (and see p. 109).

Lifting

Being disabled can affect the whole way a person thinks, as well as making it hard for her to do things for herself. Nobody enjoys not being able to get about, being dependent upon help for getting in and out of bed, on and off the loo or in and out of the bath. If you are responsible for moving your dependant, encourage her to help as much as she can.

Handling a handicapped person safely requires considerable physical skill and the wrong approach can injure you, and your dependant. Always ask the district nurse for guidance. An understanding of the 'art' of handling can save back strain and frustration for both carer and dependant. You cannot know too much about lifting techniques. Inquire whether the St John Ambulance or the British Red Cross have classes on home nursing to which you can go. If they do, then you must try to attend.

The basic principle of lifting properly is, wherever possible, to use the handicapped person's weight to advantage: just changing the position of an arm or a leg, or both, will change the body's weight distribution.

Learn what limitations the handicapped person has and how much help you can expect from her. Before you start to move or lift somebody, try to work out how best to tackle the problem (see p. 107). Careful planning of every move will be worth the time and possibly prevent you injuring yourself. Even though she may take a lot of encouraging and coaxing, the handicapped person must be encouraged to do her bit as far as she can. Doing her part will make her feel less of a burden, and will be very helpful to you and make your job easier. When you are moving her position, try to move together, so more energy will go into the move and make it less strenuous.

The carer should be familiar with the basic holds and lifts:

- moving the disabled person to the side of the bed
- getting her into bed
- getting her to sit and move up the bed
- assisting her to sit on the side of the bed
- getting her into a standing position
- raising her from sitting to lying
- helping her with walking (do not forget that a rubber-tipped walking stick, a tripod or zimmer frame may be a useful support with walking (see p. 31)
- helping her to cope with a wheelchair and stairs.

Fear of falling causes very old people to be more unsure of these movements than their infirmity necessitates, but their fear is real and they can quickly lose confidence in your support and fall.

In severe cases where you feel that the load is just too much, you may have to use a mechanical hoist. If you need a hoist ask the district nurse, or ask at the hospital if your dependant has come out or attends a day hospital.

Making the bed

- Get all the items you will need – sheets, underblanket, pillows and pillow cases, two top blankets plus an eiderdown in winter, or alternatively a duvet, if this is preferred.
- Help the old person out of the bed.
- Strip the bed.
- Put the underblanket over the mattress, or a Kylie sheet if she's incontinent.
- Put the sheet on squarely, and tuck it in along the head, then at the foot and make tidy. (Use what are called mitred corners. Ask the district nurse to show you.)
- Put on the pillows with fresh cases.
- Put on the top sheet, leaving some turnover.
- Tuck in the sheet at the foot.
- Put on the blankets, and so on.

If the dependant is in the bed you should:

- Get the items ready (as above).
- Loosen the bedclothes.
- Remove the top blanket. Fold it and put it on a chair by the bed.
- Slide the top sheet from under the second blanket and put on the chair.
- Keep her covered with the blanket.
- Roll her to one side. If you are making the bed alone, it is easier if the bed is close to – but not hard against – the wall.
- Rub out any crinkles.
- Lean and roll the layer of sheet up to her back, then roll the underblanket up to her back.
- Unroll.
- Repeat from the other side.

- Replace top sheet and take away the blanket from under the sheet.
- Tuck in the sheet. Put on the blankets, and so on.
- Gently sit her forward and plump her pillows.

The Final Stages of Your Caring

When you are caring for someone who is seriously ill and he deteriorates into the final stages, you will have to cope with his fears as well as your own distress. When he first recognizes that the end is drawing close, he may suffer disbelief and shock. He may react physically, perhaps with rapid pulse, restlessness or confusion, and need to have you close at all times. Sometimes he may become very upset, even have crying spells, or fight the inevitable and blame others for what is quite unavoidable, or become depressed. Some other very old people accept impending death almost as though they are pleased the end is near after a wearying time. At this time, believers find their religious beliefs comforting. They can give strength and courage to face death with dignity. Non-believers will find their philosophy on life and dying reassuring. If no professionals or others are available, you will be the one to help him through one or many of these stages. Gone are the days when there is always going to be an old family member reassuringly there to sit with you. Often you will have to cope alone.

With modern drugs, no patient ought to be in pain at the end, so ask the general practitioner to ensure that your loved one is not having to cope with pain, and stay by the bedside to give reassurance. Hold his hand, or place your hand gently on his forehead, and reassure him that you will not go and leave him. Right through the final stages you must endeavour to keep him clean. If he is incontinent, keep him well washed and apply barrier cream. Clean his mouth. Give adequate fluids. Help with his toilet.

At the very end his breathing may become laboured and noisy. He may become drowsy, lose consciousness, or stay conscious to the last. The physical and emotional strain on you will be great, so try to make sure you have someone else there to relieve you. If you cannot bear to leave him, sleep on a comfortable chair in the room, but eat and drink what you can to keep up your strength.

When death finally comes, close his eyelids and spend a few quiet moments with him. Then call the general practitioner. At this time you really ought not to be alone. Even though you may have expected him to die you will be shocked and distressed. All sorts of feelings may come to the surface: terrible sadness, anger that he has left you, guilt that perhaps you did not do enough, or were brittle the day before when you were exhausted and distressed. You will tend to think back, to wish you had said so many things and not said so many things. You can take some comfort in the knowledge that all of us have similar feelings to one degree or another. In the longer term you will be greatly comforted if you know in your heart that you did your best.

During bereavement, you will have to make some important decisions about your future –

- how to cope financially
- if you are under retirement age, whether to go back to work (you may need a refresher course)
- whether or when to move house
- getting back into a normal life pattern.

Do not make any decision without due thought. Consult friends, relatives or professionals. If you are tired, try to take a holiday. Getting back to work can alleviate loneliness, help you to make friends and increase your income – it will be worth the effort. Although we advise this, we do recognize that it may not be easy to get a job at a time of high unemployment.

CHAPTER 9

Coping with Dependency

In many cases the caring load will be greatly alleviated if you work out a system. Seek to maintain a positive attitude; acknowledge your own limitations and do not let yourself become self-dependent. Track down and use voluntary and statutory resources and personnel. Try to understand what particular pressures can build up in what circumstances, and plan ahead so that you get long-term and short-term breaks.

The action you decide to take when your parent can no longer cope will be governed by several factors. Among them will be:

- your love for and relationship with her (perhaps she was not much of a parent to you when you were young)
- your sense of responsibility towards her
- how near you live to her
- how much money (income and capital) each of you has
- your house and her house – the style and size
- your career or other family commitments (you may have a disabled husband or child or a handful of small children, or a husband and children whom you have spoilt and who will resent sharing your attention)
- your own health
- just how bad she really is, and what services there are where she lives.

Your decisions may not be easy. You will probably weigh up:

- what reactions the rest of the family, friends and neighbours will have if you decide not to look after her
- how guilty you will feel if you opt out (you may even think about whether you will miss out on a legacy or her house if you refuse to accept responsibility for her care).

Then you will have to decide whether:

- to leave her where she is and care for her from a distance
- to stay at work and care for her
- to leave work and stay at home
- to go back home and live with her
- to take her to live with you
- to arrange for her to go into sheltered housing
- to arrange for her to go into a nursing home or residential care.

In this chapter we have outlined these possibilities for caring, sometimes using case histories for illustration, so that you can decide which type of carer you are.

Living Arrangements for Older People

A short case history will set the scene.

Betty's father has suddenly died. Her mother is now left on her own in a big house with a large garden, down in Dorset. Betty works in London. She is forty-nine, and her mother is seventy-five and has had arthritis, but she can still look after herself. Betty's father shopped, did the garden and vacuumed the house. Her mother is shattered by his death. They have been very close. Betty goes down every weekend. She does not want to go home to stay, and she knows her mother will not be happy in London. Her mother has good neighbours and a circle of friends. In trying to come to a decision about what to do, Betty should recognize that:

- Grief can mar her judgement, and she will see her mother grieving and feel she cannot just leave her alone.
- Given encouragement, extra time and affection, her mother will probably settle down gradually to her changed life.
- It is her mother who ought to decide what she wants. Perhaps she has relied so much on her husband emotionally that she will not be able to live there alone. She should just be sure that no decisions are taken too quickly.
- Her mother may not want to leave her friends and neighbourhood and house. A house is more than bricks and mortar; it holds many memories. If these memories are happy, they will be part of the surviving person's identity.
- A short break away with a friend or a relative, staying a couple of weeks, may help her mother to accept what has happened.
- She should try not to be pressured by what other family or friends say or might think.
- She will be reassured if she talks to her mother's doctor and makes sure that she can cope physically.

If her mother decides to stay put, there are other possible ways to help her which can be considered:

- Her mother may be able to close off part of the house.
- She could perhaps take in a student for company.
- She may decide to pay a redundant older person or an unemployed young person to come in and do the garden and odd jobs.
- Neighbours, the milkman and the postman can be contacted.
- Her reassurance that they will be in constant contact will give her mother more confidence.

- A telephone is a must, if she can afford it.
- An alarm system is desirable, if it is within her means, to give her a sense of security.
- Security locks and chains can be attached to the doors and windows.
- The gas cooker can be checked by British Gas without charge.
- The electric wiring can be checked by the Electricity Board, who will do a free visual check and put in a fire extinguisher.
- A few simple installations, such as lights over the stairs, will make the house safer.
- The house can be checked for trailing electric flexes and for torn lino and ragged carpet ends which could cause accidents.
- The taps can be changed so that her arthritic hands can manage them better.
- Rails can be put in beside the bath and loo.
- There are special kitchen gadgets to make kitchen chores less difficult. (The occupational therapist can be asked about rails, gadgets and aids.)
- A carefully worked out budget will keep her mother from worrying about money.
- She may be able to raise income on a home loan scheme (see p. 153); or by taking in a tenant or a lodger. If she takes in a tenant, she ought to be aware of tenants' rights and the difficulty in getting them out; and she should remember that there may be a resulting tax liability when the house is finally sold – the bank manager can advise on this. Despite these points of caution, she may still choose to take someone in so that she will not be lonely.
- The neighbours can be given a duplicate key.
- A lot of her shopping can be done in bulk by relatives, which will just leave her with having to carry perishables – and

shopping for those will have the advantage of getting her out and about.

- She may be entitled to some financial help from state benefits (check leaflet HB1).
- A home help (see p. 101), or a cleaner paid for privately by her mother or herself, will be an advantage.
- It may be sensible to have a loo and bathroom put in downstairs (see p. 30).
- It is important to encourage other members of the family to help. Often grandchildren love to go and stay during their holidays.
- It is necessary for her mother to feel that she is making a real contribution, and Betty should accept her mother's knitted garments, her pot-pourri, her jam with the gratitude and pleasure they deserve.
- It is vital not to stop constant visits abruptly. She should gradually increase the gaps between the visits so her mother will not feel hurt. After a few weeks she will probably be busy again, and will not need Betty so often.
- Betty should accept that she may refer continuously to her father, as that may be how she is dealing with her loss.
- Meals on wheels may later help her to stay put.
- Sheltered housing may be an alternative if things do not settle down or she needs more support.

Working and Caring

Although some carers manage not to give up their jobs, they can become exhausted by the added burden of anxiety about what is happening at home while they are at work. This anxiety is bound to affect the quality of a carer's work. It may stop her from accepting promotion or a different job offer, because she cannot cope with the added responsibility, or she is not able to travel or move. By continuing to work she will have financial security, but perhaps at the expense of her health.

Because she is still earning, the carer ought to be able to 'buy in' services which are not available at statutory and voluntary level. She should use the attendance allowance, where it is available, to pay for sitters-in either during the day or evenings. Against the financial advantage must be weighed various problems which the carer may experience. She may feel very guilty if she socializes in the evenings or at weekends. On the other hand, staying at work will mean she will not become socially isolated and intra-dependent. Caring will not be her whole raison d'être, so resentment should not surface. If the carer is married, however, there will almost certainly be the demands of children, spouse *and* dependant to cope with after work.

To prevent the old person's social isolation, the carer can pay sitters-in, leave her a television or radio, arrange for her to go to a day centre or lunch club, or to visit her friends if this is practicable.

The carer can try to organize her life so she spaces out the chores and she has time to unwind on her own and time to spend with the old person. Remember that, if she has been alone, she is going to be hungry for the carer's company. The carer's life and what is going on in the world outside will be exciting news to her, however mundane it may seem to the carer, and she will want to tell the carer about her day. If patience begins to ebb, a carer should think back to when she was at school and her mother listened to her day's doings.

When a carer feels she can no longer cope because:

- she needs more support
- she is too exhausted to carry on
- she knows that her career is at a critical stage and she will be

resentful if she passes over an important opportunity – then she should weigh up the options of sheltered housing if it is feasible. (Ask Age Concern, Anchor, or Abbeyfield about this accommodation (see p. 131), a nursing home, or residential care.)

For lists of privately run, inspected nursing homes in the London area contact Counsel and Care for the Elderly (p. 161) or GRACE (p. 162).

Giving up Work to Care

Carers may feel they have to give up their work to look after an aged infirm or disabled spouse, parent or parent-in-law. Sons or daughters who have always lived at home may believe they have to leave work to care full-time. Before taking this step they should ask:

- whether the relative's condition really warrants full-time care – check with the general practitioner
- whether there are any other services or persons who could be brought in to support the old person.
- whether the relative is claiming all the allowances and benefits for which he or she may qualify too pay for help.

Before making a final decision, they should talk to a professional, who may well suggest such ideas as:

- a home help
- the district nurse
- meals on wheels
- the old person attending a day centre
- paying someone to keep an eye on the old person.

These could be some of the consequences of giving up work:

- In the short term, income will be lost, and even savings used up.
- In general, a married woman or one who is co-habiting does not qualify for invalid care allowance.
- A person who would qualify will have to wait for a period of six months before receiving any money, since this is the time for which a person has to be in need of care before claiming the attendance allowance. Invalid care allowance is not payable unless the person being cared for receives the attendance allowance, for which qualifying requirements are stringent.
- Long-term income will be reduced, because the occupational pension will be less.
- Chances of getting back into employment will be affected.

Work out in advance who will pay for what. Housing may become a problem later: mortgage payments may not be possible, savings may be chiselled away, and the old person may leave her house to someone else or make no provision even for a life tenancy. People who leave work in order to care may tend to decide they can cope without the support services, and end up exhausting themselves. They may not feel able to keep up their social contacts, and find that they let them slide. Some married couples never get out together; some single carers are essentially housebound with their relative.

There are other problems which must be considered:

- a marriage can have a strain put on it when a parent or parent-in-law is being cared for
- the old person might feel guilty and the carer resentful, and together they will create a strained atmosphere
- a carer who leaves her independence behind will have to adapt to living at home again

- carers who are part of a couple will lose the comfort and enjoyment of their sex life if a partner becomes disabled
- domestic role reversal is never easy, and it may cause tensions.

These negative aspects of caring are listed to give you an idea of what you can expect – understanding them will help you to cope better. There are some people who end up caring, not because they really want to accept the responsibility for looking after someone, but because they are tired of work. What they do not realize is that they may be getting into a far heavier workload. Those who use caring as a cover for leaving work are likely to be people:

- who have no job satisfaction
- who do not make friends easily
- who feel secure at home
- who have a low self-image
- who are in their forties, have never married, and who feel that they have been at work long enough – a most understandable attitude perhaps, but short-sighted

By leaving work, such people can get off the treadmill and settle back into the cocoon of home. When the caring becomes difficult, however, such carers will generally become resentful, and feel caught up in something for which they have no sense of vocation.

Carers Who Are Retired

As more people live to an advanced age, carers themselves are often over retirement age. If you are in this category, you will face certain problems, and you may have negative reactions:

- You feel your own years are slipping by, and you can see no light at the end of the tunnel.
- Your own retirement plans – your 'golden years' – the time you were going to do all those special things – are shattered, and you can feel frustrated and resentful.
- Any thoughts of a second career and perhaps a higher income or pension have to be shelved.
- Caring can be very physically wearying for people who have the beginnings of disability themselves.
- Seeing someone who is not that much older than you deteriorate can cause anxiety about what is going to happen to you. A woman, particularly, can find herself caring for an older husband and a very old parent at the same time.
- You can become socially isolated and exhausted.

If you are retired and caring for someone, think especially about planning, knowing what to expect, learning what support exists in your area, and using it.

Taking the Relative to Live with You

For this move to be successful, the carer must do a lot of advance thinking. Here are some of the questions which a carer ought to consider before she brings her relative to live with her:

- How will the old person adapt to a house that is not his, to a neighbourhood that is not his, and to the absence of friends and familiar faces?
- Will the carer's accommodation be large enough to give them both privacy?
- If the carer has children, just how thoughtful and adaptable are they?

- For how long and to what stage of disability does the carer believe she will be able to cope?

There are some positive steps that you can take in an effort to see that things work out:

- If you are married, have a family conference – talk about the pros and cons.
- If you are single, be sure you are willing to give up your privacy and some of your independent life style.
- Financial decisions should be sorted out – decide who will pay for what. Make sure that the old person is never put in a back room, unless that is the only place, and particularly not if he has pooled his savings to buy a bigger house so that he can move in with you.
- See that the old person's room is as comfortable, bright and pretty as possible, and let him bring some of his own possessions to furnish it.
- Try to involve him in the decision-making and the choices. He still has favourite foods, programmes and friends. Do not expect him to fit in completely with your ways.
- Mutual respect of privacy is essential. Children must knock before going into his place, and he ought not to interfere if their friends are with them or your friends are visiting, unless he is invited.
- Encourage him to keep up those interests which are feasible.
- Try to keep to the normal routine and comings and goings as far as possible.
- When they are needed, bring in the support services (see p. 88).
- Encourage other family members to visit him and take their turn at looking after him while you get a break.
- Bear in mind that, later on, sheltered accommodation or a nursing home may be necessary.

Mutual respect of privacy and life styles is the key to making this arrangement work out.

Nursing Homes and Residential Care

Admitting a dependent old person to a nursing home or place of residential care can be a traumatic time for both carer and old person. The dependant will probably feel let down; the carer will almost certainly feel guilty.

These factors may lead to the old person's admission:

- the dependant's decision not to be cared for by the family
- their incompatibility
- the carer's need to stay at work
- the carer's poor health
- the dependant's deteriorating condition
- the carer's exhaustion from caring
- sheltered accommodation not being suitable for the dependant.

If the dependant is going to a residential place of care, her carer should:

- talk to her about it
- check on what the policy will be if she suddenly becomes confused or incontinent
- where feasible, take her to see the place and note the atmosphere
- check what kind of care is available, and find out the ratio of staff to patients
- make sure she will be encouraged to be as independent as possible and not worn down by routine
- be reassuring

- visit her often until she settles in, so that she will not feel abandoned
- take along whatever treasures she is allowed
- encourage her to take part in activities.

The advantages are that she will not have to worry about budgeting, house or garden maintenance, or becoming a burden on her family. You will be able to keep her in touch with news of family and friends, keep her looking nice and ensure that she is properly cared for.

If you neglect her, or refuse to provide for the old person out of assets over which you have receivership through the Court of Protection, or abandon her, you are bound to have to cope with guilt after her death; that guilt can be very difficult to come to terms with.

Your interests could be affected, because if you are to benefit under the will, and a charge has been put on the house to repay the local authority for having taken the old person into care, it will have to be paid out of the estate. That could mean that the house will have to be sold. You will have to weigh up your exhaustion against the old person's right to proper care. In coming to your conclusion you will therefore have to decide how you will meet any accrued charges, without being put in the position of having to sell the parental home. Counsel and Care for the Elderly can advise on choosing a suitable nursing home in the London area (see p. 161), and on financial aspects. There are local authority, voluntary and private homes. The social worker will arrange for admission to a local authority home. Voluntary and private homes suit persons who do not require full-time care. Age Concern (see p. 160) has a leaflet on charging procedures.

CHAPTER 10

The Special Problems of Those Who Do the Caring

The relationship between you the carer and the person (or persons) for whom you are caring is vital. Each of you is an individual and has needs. Your general attitude is all-important.

That attitude will be influenced by your relationship with the old person, how you begin, what support you receive and, particularly, what respite or breaks away you get. So that you will not begin to feel over-burdened, trapped or exhausted, you must see your caring as a partnership with the voluntary and statutory support system.

Your parent's attitude will be affected by how she has accepted being dependent, by her long-standing relationship with you, and by the way in which external support is introduced.

This chapter is intended to give you some insight into how you and she may feel and react, and to offer some helpful solutions. We hope that at the end of the day you will be able to say, 'Thank God I did it.'

Your Approach

When you begin to care, do not organize your attitudes and your life style around the belief that you will not be caring for all that long. Time will pass and patterns you have set up will invariably become established and be hard to break. Remember that none of us knows for how long anyone will survive. The doctors may make an educated guess, but even they cannot say for certain. Therefore it is important to adopt the overall attitude that, as you do not know how long you will have the responsibility, you must organize your life to cope with·it. Caring is a job and it is an art. It can be done well or poorly. It can give satisfaction or it can produce a miserable condition. Do not become a carer if you do not like your parent or if he or she does not like you. Things will not change – life-long attitudes can only get worse. You may feel guilt pangs, but these are to be preferred to bitter recriminations and to both of you leading doggedly wretched lives.

If you do decide to care, approach the role on the basis of making her life more tolerable and comfortable, and of keeping your own independence as far as you can. Where it is possible to do so, try to compartmentalize your approach. Introduce a flexible caring pattern right from the start – learn what to do and what support is available. Don't just plough on, getting exhausted, muddled and dreading the next day. Be organized, plan ahead as far as you are able. Of course, in cases which are terminal or where the old person is severely demented, you will not be able to plan so readily, but at this stage (in most cases) you should have your back-up team sorted out. You have to know where to find support (see p. 79), and how far you can expect to rely on that support.

It is very important not to allow your dependant to become more dependent than she has to be. A case history illustrates this.

Sarah B's mother breaks her hip, and the consultant recommends physiotherapy twice a week to get her on her feet quickly. Mrs B refuses to co-operate and becomes virtually chairbound. Sarah sympathizes with her and does not encourage her to work at getting going again. Mrs B becomes dependent when she does not have to, and Sarah has made an unnecessary rod for her own back.

It is vital to encourage independence whenever you can. One of the difficulties in caring for a parent is that your very special relationship with them has built up barriers which have been there a lifetime, and which are not easy to cross. It is hard to say to your parent, 'Look, you really can dress yourself', or, 'You will be able to walk – Dr Green said there's just no medical reason why you can't.'

Do not 'baby' her. You will be unkind if you do, because you will probably be robbing her of the one thing she has left – human dignity. If you do 'baby' her, you will be meeting *your* urge to feel wanted, and not her actual need.

Some old people take to their beds without real cause. If she does not seem ill and yet will not get up, call the general practitioner immediately. He may even need to refer her to a psychiatrist. Do not rely on old wives' tales or what someone down the road thinks is wrong, or accept that she is different because she is getting old. Get the general practitioner to make a thorough examination. Ask questions about the condition and what can be done about it, and about just how helpless your parent should really be or will become. It is in her best interests to keep her involved, as far as her health allows.

If your parent is still mobile, even if she is slightly confused, delegate some duties or jobs to her. For instance, get her to take part in some light dusting, doing the drying up, peeling the potatoes, or folding the towels. This will stop her from sitting too long and getting wrapped up in her solitude, and she will derive satisfaction from the knowledge that she is still contributing.

Illness can make a person who once enjoyed company shun people, and she will feel just as cut off and isolated as you will. At first she may resist people coming in because she fears you will tend to neglect her needs. But if you persevere she will generally end up accepting them, liking them, and not feeling so out of things.

Finances and work

In view of the fact that she will have moved in with you, or you back with her, a fair amount of upheaval will have taken place. You may first find it difficult to discuss some subjects, and they may be important ones, such as how to work out your finances. As soon as you agree to care for her, or as soon as the subject can be decently approached, some arrangement should be made about money. It is never a good idea to let the whole topic go unmentioned, because then ill-feeling results. Some old people become very acquisitive, bank every penny they get their hands on, and refuse to contribute towards the upkeep of the house or themselves. Some who receive the attendance allowance refuse to part with any part of it. They regard their care as the carer's duty, and will not budge from that viewpoint. Therefore it is essential, wherever possible, for the subject to be discussed right at the beginning, so that finances can be put into their proper perspective. Assuming responsibility for her care may stir up some conflicts for you, and they will be emotionally wearying. If you are working, it will be hard for you to give your full attention to your work. Conflicts of loyalty may arise and make you edgy, possibly even resentful. If you have a husband and family (and perhaps even a sick husband or child to care for also) you may feel as though you do not know which way to turn, as your attention and love will be needed by so many.

Changed roles

Caring invariably means a change in roles. Instead of your parent being responsible for you, you become responsible for her, and she may dig her heels in and refuse to go along with what you want her to do. Her attitude could possibly become: 'Why, the impertinence of you, a mere youngster (despite the fact that you are sixty) telling me to take medicine or use a frame to walk to the toilet.' You will need patience, but gently and firmly explain that you must have her co-operation if you are to be responsible for her. If she persists in being difficult, ask her doctor to talk to her. It is amazing how readily what the doctor suggests is acceptable. You may find that there has to be a scene, which will of course be upsetting, but if it clears the air you should both have a better opportunity to work things out.

It is worth reminding yourself that if your parent was always a thoughtful person she will almost certainly stay that way, unless her whole personality is damaged by severe disability – either physical or mental. Dementia can produce difficult changes which a carer can hardly believe (see p. 79). The only way to deal with these changes is to hope that people will accept that they are caused by illness and not be offended or shocked. You are bound to be hurt if she accuses you of theft or of longing to poison her, even though you recognize full well that she does not know what she is saying and that if she was in her right mind she would be horrified at herself. If you have never spoken affectionately to one another in the past, you cannot complain that anything new is going on now, on the other hand, and a family 'doormat' suddenly finding herself the centre of attention may enjoy the role and make herself appear more helpless than she really is. It is not at all unusual for a parent to adopt a 'holier than thou' attitude while others are around and be virtually impossible to live with when the outsider has gone. We all know of the difficult old folk who say and do all the right things when the doctor or the vicar calls! Don't be a Jekyll and Hyde yourself.

Keeping your own identity

Dependants can become selfish. Do not let your time, attention or affection be possessed by her. If she is disabled she may be inclined to put her own needs before yours, blotting out your need for company of your own age, and interests of your own. Her behaviour can be called the 'survival ploy'. If this happens, talk to her kindly and firmly and tell her that you must have some life of your own, even as she, at your own age, had her freedom. Maintaining your freedom and independence depends to a large degree on your determination to keep up your interests and social contacts as far as you can.

Your life may become so closely combined with hers that you get frustrated. Frustration can take lots of forms – it can make you depressed, restless or fed up, and it can even affect your health. It can lead to destructive bitterness which eats away at your whole outlook on life. No one wants an embittered and whining person around them.

When other family members come to visit, even if they have not shown their faces around the door for years, she will generally greet them happily and sing their praises for days after they have gone. You may well feel hurt and jealous, even angry, because there you are with all the responsibility, with your whole life quite possibly governed by her needs. You look and feel tired and on a treadmill; they arrive fresh and relaxed, bearing gifts, full of news of all their exciting doings, so different from your own conversation, and then they go off and she weeps and clings to their every expression and word.

If you have a martyrish attitude, you may hide behind it and blame the old person's influence, when in fact you yourself enjoy being put upon. Or if you never liked to be away from the cocoon of your family and felt insecure, you may make the excuse of not being able to get out. In these cases you will not really rebel against being dominated. If you want to change, you must talk to your doctor about your attitudes, because you may need help from a trained counsellor.

If you don't bother to have other people around because, for instance, you will have to clear up the house before they come in, you will be depriving yourself of important support. You risk keeping yourself socially isolated, and you will be robbing your parent of different company and a break in what could be a monotonous routine. Remember that she probably grows as weary of just seeing you as you do of being alone with her. Of course things will not be easy, and they can be jolly difficult, even downright mentally and physically exhausting for much of the time; but no job is ever entirely problem-free, and we all get fed up from time to time. We would not be human if we didn't.

Finding help

It is the way in which you tackle the difficulties that is important. There are voluntary and statutory bodies and professionals who can advise and guide you and put you in touch with help. They will direct you to people and places where short-term and long-term breaks can be arranged, to give you a rest. There are statutory, voluntary and private sector respite services. At the statutory level, we have many more social services sitter-in schemes to give you a break, and the National Health Service has some hospital beds available. At the voluntary level, hundreds of respite services have sprung up. Inquire at Age Concern, the Volunteer Bureau, the Citizens' Advice Bureau or the National Council for Carers and their Elderly Dependants. At the private sector level, there are some excellent schemes at rates much lower than you would have to pay a fully qualified nurse (whom you generally do not need) from a nursing agency.

In some parts of the country services are not as good as in others. If a statutory service is not available, inquire at the Citizens' Advice Bureau whether there is a voluntary service to help you. If you do not ask, you will not know just what is there.

You must not let yourself become enveloped in caring to the

exclusion of everything else. It can be so easy to get into the position of not wanting to go out. Sadly, some carers then get depressed, develop health problems and become social misfits. Never let yourself get into a state of neglect.

Keep up your contacts and interests. Anyone who can read and write ought never to be lonely or just have to sit around – there are so many interesting things in life, and not all of them cost money. The library service is free, the radio is a constant source of entertainment and interest, there is the garden, handicrafts, homecrafts . . . the list is endless. Everyone has some talents, and if you have previously worked full-time you may not have developed yours, owing to lack of time and energy. At home you have a certain amount of control over your routine.

If you feel at the end of your tether, you must go and seek help. Do not wait until the crisis stage. Violence against anyone is not acceptable, and least of all against a helpless old person. Remember that it is normal to get upset, lose your temper and say things you regret, but physical abuse is intolerable. It is a criminal offence and you could well be charged with assault or worse. If you are violently disposed, or frustrated and bitter because you have not made anything of your life, do not take it out on a helpless or demented old person who does not realize what she is doing.

Recognizing Your Limitations

A lot of carers feel that they are the only ones who can look after someone close to them. After all, they may say, they know her likes and dislikes. And they may become set in the idea that only they can cope, or as reliant on the need to care as the old person is on them doing the caring, so that they will find it extraordinarily difficult to allow someone else to take over. That someone else may be close family, friends, professionals or volunteers. If you begin to feel this way, ask yourself whether you are resisting because:

- you have come to feel so indispensable
- you are afraid that she will react angrily and it won't be worth a scene
- you are her favourite human being and you are afraid someone else will edge into that enviable position
- you are her most favoured beneficiary and you stand to inherit quite a bit
- you dearly want her to admire you and to need your help.

Whatever the real reason, remember you will find it increasingly difficult to introduce someone new the longer the caring goes on. People will get tired of offering if you constantly refuse. You yourself will become bogged down and less amenable to change, and your health could suffer in the end.

When you have weighed everything up, if you do decide to take action to get relief, you may be met by anger and by outbursts such as: 'I never left you when you were small, but you go and enjoy yourself.' You may encounter instances of emotional blackmail: 'I could be dead by the time you get back, or be lying here with broken bones.' Or possessiveness: 'I thought you loved me ... I don't like being left with other people ... that friend of yours doesn't really care about you. I won't rest a minute while you're away.' Nearly everyone would react to such statements. We could feel annoyance at the selfishness, and some guilt or anxiety while we are in fact not there.

As a carer you may find your patience wearing thin with other people's attitudes to your parent. Sadly, there are insensitive people around who almost shout when they address an old person, or get impatient and upset them unnecessarily, or speak to them as though they are children. 'And how is Old Granny today?' can be terribly insulting to an old dignified lady with all her wits about her. She is bound to feel like a second-rate citizen.

Chapters 6 and 7 discuss mental illness and confused behaviour in detail; both can be very trying, and you should always seek help if you are having trouble. Sexual aggression can be a problem with some confused old people (see p. 90). They may compare the carer with a deceased spouse or lover and make sexual overtures. Particularly to a single daughter or son, such behaviour can be most upsetting. It will often happen at bath time, and because the carer is embarrassed about it, it will not be mentioned to any professional. As with so many aspects of dementia, the carer must accept the behaviour as the result of disease, and try not to be too shocked by it.

Depression

Although depression is normal (see Chapter 6), coping with an elderly person's depression can be wearying, especially if there are just the two of you in the house. A bleak attitude to everything and everyone eventually rubs off, and however bright you are determined to be, you will probably end up feeling pretty low in spirits yourself.

There are many possible causes of depression:

- losing a spouse or friends
- having a severe disability
- feeling insecure about the future
- worrying about making ends meet
- illness or other misfortune in the family.

If the old person becomes withdrawn, paints everything in shades of black or grey, and just sits refusing to be interested in things or people, take it as a sign of the onset of depression, and talk to the general practitioner. It could be that the old person has an infection or that the attitude is due to the side-effects of drugs. Or perhaps it is a problem which a psychogeriatrician can cure. A professional's intervention will prevent the condition from getting worse and making the dependant miserable, and your own life dreary. To help, you will have to give all your love and understanding, because if the old person is to be well again he must feel secure and wanted.

A negative-sounding or difficult person can keep people away. Don't forget that either of you can be at fault. Visitors will stop calling if they only hear the bleak side of life, so if you are to keep yourself and him from becoming socially isolated he and you (if you realize you are sinking into depression) must get medical help.

It is a fact that men are not very good at dealing with illness. They generally shrink from visiting their sick friends. If your father is disabled or infirm, you may virtually have to bribe his friends to visit him. But once they relax and settle in you will probably find it hard to get them out of the house. If your father can get along, aided or unaided, do not stop him from going next door or to the pub to see his male friends. If his morale is kept up he will cope better with his disability.

Guilt

Guilt can be destructive. There are any number of possible causes:

- a child or spouse not wanting to do the caring
- a deep-seated wish to be freed from the whole set-up
- a nagging urge to go back to a career and to leave your dependant to look after herself
- agreeing to put the old person into residential care
- not contributing towards the old person's upkeep, when you could do so

- all the 'if onlys' which come back when the old person dies
- having felt anger and lost your temper.

Health can be seriously affected by long periods of guilt feelings, and if the feelings persist, you should consult your general practitioner. Guilt is not inevitable: it can be avoided by striking a realistic balance between the needs of the carer and those of the dependant. The balance will bring a rewarding and happy relationship.

CHAPTER 11

Benefits and Allowances

To obtain fuller information on benefits and allowances, you should go to the DHSS or tax office.

Attendance Allowance

What is it?

The attendance allowance is payable to a person who is severely disabled, either physically or mentally, and who has needed a certain level of care for at least six months.

It is not means-tested, and the person getting it need not have paid national insurance contributions. It is tax-free and paid in addition to any other benefits or income. The allowance is paid at two rates: the higher rate and the lower rate.

How much care must someone need to qualify?

The person claiming the allowance must need frequent attention throughout the day in connection with bodily functions (such as help with turning in bed, getting out of bed, washing all over, washing hair, shaving, going to the loo, dressing, eating, drinking, and so on).

The person claiming must need this help 'throughout' the day, not just first thing in the morning and last thing at night. Or she must need constant supervision to prevent danger to herself or others, or repeated or prolonged attention during the night in connection with her bodily functions, or continued supervision throughout the night to avoid substantial danger to herself and others.

The higher rate is paid if the person needs attention during the day *and* night. The lower rate is paid if the person needs attention during the day *or* night.

It is not necessary for anyone in the household to give up work before it is paid. If the application is not successful the first time, apply a second or even a third time.

How to claim

A completed social security form N1205 should be sent to the local social security office. A covering letter can be attached if you feel that more information will support the claim. The claimant will then be given a medical examination by a physician at home. The Attendance Allowance Board will then notify the claimant of its decision by post.

Who gets the allowance?

The sick or disabled person gets the allowance.

If, however, he cannot get out to cash the payment, he can arrange for someone to cash it for him. Or when he cannot manage his own affairs because of illness or a mental condition, the allowance will be paid to the carer or to whoever else is authorized to act legally on his behalf.

Change in circumstances

A person who normally lives in a hospital or local authority accommodation will not be entitled to the allowance. But if he goes home for holidays and weekends, it is payable.

When someone goes into hospital or into a hostel funded by the local authority, she will continue to get the allowance for the first four weeks – provided she has been out of hospital for at least twenty-eight days.

If she goes into a local authority home, the allowance will stop after a total of four weeks.

What happens if things change – when the claimant gets worse?

If he already gets the lower rate allowance, a new application does not have to be made. Write to the Attendance Allowance Unit at the DHSS, North Fylde Central Office, Norcross, Blackpool FY5 3TA, quoting all the numbers from the form which certifies your entitlement to the allowance, and saying that you are now worse and you think you ought to get the higher rate allowance, for attendance during the day and night. The unit will get a further report from the doctor.

If the review succeeds, the higher rate will be back-dated to the week you asked for the review.

Invalid Care Allowance

What is it?

An allowance payable to certain persons of working age who cannot work because they have to stay at home to care for an elderly disabled person.

Who qualifies?

If you are caring for a severely disabled person at home and you are not a married woman being maintained by your husband (but check the leaflet for details) or a co-habiting woman, and you are between sixteen and sixty (for a woman) or sixteen and sixty-five (for a man), if you live in the UK, spend at least thirty-five hours a week caring for the person, and are not working or on a course of full-time education, you will receive the allowance, if the person for whom you are caring gets the attendance allowance. The allowance carries a Class I contribution credit for your national insurance record.

If you cannot claim because you are a married woman living with your husband, or are co-habiting, or if you are separated and are receiving a certain amount of maintenance from your husband – then you should claim home responsibilities protection to preserve your pension rights.

How to claim

Obtain leaflet NI212 from a social security office, and forward the attached form to: The Controller, Invalid Care Allowance Unit, Central Office, Norcross, Blackpool FY5 3TA.

What else should you know?

If you receive the allowance you can earn up to £12 a week without losing your entitlement to benefit. You can deduct certain expenses from the gross sum. These are: fares to work, tools and equipment, excessive wear and tear of normal clothing, the cost of any meal taken during working hours up to a specified value (provided your employer does not issue Luncheon Vouchers) and the cost of providing for the necessary care of a member of the household during your absence at work. (Write to the social security office for the full list of deductible expenses.)

Invalidity Benefit

Who qualifies?

Note that there are two elements. Persons who are still incapable of work when their sickness benefit ends may go on to invalidity benefit. Persons who become chronically ill before reaching the age of sixty (men) or fifty-five (women) will receive invalidity allowance as well as invalidity pension.

How to claim

The claimant should send the statements provided by her general practitioner to the local social security office. Leaflet NII6A gives more details about invalidity benefit.

Mobility Allowance

What is it?

A non-means-tested cash benefit to help severely disabled persons become more mobile. It is not taxable.

Who qualifies?

The claimant must not have reached his or her sixty-sixth birthday. On qualifying, a person may be paid the benefit until the age of seventy-five, provided that he or she meets certain other conditions. These conditions are that he or she is unable or virtually unable to walk because of a physical condition and likely to remain so for at least a year. The claimant must be a UK resident and must actually be able to use the allowance.

If a claimant goes abroad permanently the allowance will cease.

If you go into hospital you will still receive the allowance, if you can benefit from it.

How to claim

Fill in the form with leaflet NI2I I, which you can get from the social security office. If you already get the attendance allowance (or any other allowance for which a medical examination was necessary) you may get the mobility allowance without a further examination; otherwise you must have one.

Home Responsibilities Protection

What is it?

It protects your pension rights if you are not making national insurance contributions because you are at home for a whole tax year looking after someone and not receiving a benefit (such as the Invalid Care Allowance) which credits you with contributions. The scheme started in April 1978, so only the tax years after that time will be covered by home responsibilities protection.

Who qualifies?

You must spend at least thirty-five hours a week looking after someone who is receiving attendance allowance, or you must be receiving supplementary benefit so that you can look after an elderly or sick person at home.

You should carefully note these warnings:

- If you are looking after someone who gets attendance allowance and that person goes into hospital for five weeks, she will lose the attendance allowance for one week, but you will lose home responsibilities protection for a whole year. It is important to be aware of this.

- A married woman who pays the married woman's national insurance stamp cannot claim home responsibilities protection.

How to claim

See leaflet NP27, which you can get from a social security office.

Other Social Security Benefits

For information on supplementary benefit see leaflet SB1, which you can get from the social security office.

To find out about housing benefits (see p. 127) get in touch with the housing department of your local authority, and ask for a leaflet and application form.

To find out about help for handicapped people, get leaflet HB1 from the social security office.

You can get *Your Rights* and *Which Benefit* by post from Age Concern, 60 Pitcairn Road, Mitcham, Surrey CR4 3LL. They will help you to find out what older people are entitled to claim.

Improvement Grants

A home improvement grant may be given if the home lacks standard facilities (such as a bathroom, loo, or hot water system) or if extra facilities are needed because the person cannot get at the ones already there. A grant may also be available for other improvements to make a house more suitable for a disabled person's special needs.

For more information contact the improvement grant officer at the local district council offices.

Tax Allowances

Dependent relative tax allowance

This is a tax allowance which can be granted for each person related to you through birth or marriage, if you are helping to support them.

They are not required to live with you but they have to be either sixty-four or older before the start of the tax year; or older than sixteen and incapacitated by infirmity; or your widowed, separated or divorced mother-in-law.

Note that single, separated, divorced and widowed women get the higher rate.

If more than one person contributes to the relative's maintenance the allowance is approved on the basis of what each person pays.

Blind person's allowance

This is granted to you if you or your wife are registered as blind with the local authority.

Housekeeper allowance

Widows or widowers can get this if a relative or an employee lives with them and acts as a housekeeper. If the housekeeper is a son or daughter, it is better to claim this allowance, instead of the lower allowance available for a son or daughter on whose services the claimant has to depend because of age or disability.

Home Insurance Plan

An elderly home owner trying to get extra money to stay on where she is might well think about a home insurance plan.

How it works

The old person remains the owner of her house and at the same time gets income from the capital value of it. A mortgage loan is raised on a proportion of the value of the property, up to a certain maximum figure. An annuity income is bought with this sum and is paid during the purchaser's lifetime (the purchaser is called the 'annuitant'). When the purchaser dies the loan is repaid.

How to get a mortgage annuity

Talk to your banker or solicitor before you do anything. There are many schemes, and you can write for details to any major building society.

Budgeting

The table shows a simple budget formula. Extras can normally be made to fit into the budget by careful management.

Sources of Income	
For the old person	*For the carer*
retirement pension/occupational pension attendance allowance annuity/dividends	invalid care allowance *and possibly* some supple- mentary benefit *or* salary

Outgoings		
Fixed essential	*Variable essential*	*Extras*
rent/mortgage household repairs taxation	fuel food clothes telephone chemist's bills	entertainment transport holidays

Some useful tips

- set a limit for spending in each area and try to stick to it
- buy at sales
- cook more than one dish at a time in the oven
- grow vegetables if you have the chance
- make out a shopping list and stick to it
- check that you are getting all the benefits and allowances to which you are entitled.

CHAPTER 12

Legal Points

Making Out a Will

Many families are diffident about asking an aged parent to discuss legal matters, particularly making a will, from fear of seeming grasping. By the same token, old people are often reluctant to make out a will, because it reminds them that their life is coming to a close. It is a great mistake to ignore the subject on two counts:

- dying without having made out a will can cause very many problems for surviving relatives
- the old person's wishes may well not be carried out.

Go to a solicitor

Always go to a solicitor to have a will made out. The Citizens' Advice Bureau should have the address of a solicitor who will help people who do not have enough money to pay the usual fee.

Rules

Here are a few of the very basic rules which can affect the validity of a will and whether you may benefit under it:

- It must be in writing.

- It must be signed by the person making it (the testator), or by someone in her presence or by her direction, as long as it appears that the testator intended by her signature to give effect to the will.
- The testator must make or acknowledge her signature in the presence of two witnesses both present at the same time, and each witness must sign or acknowledge his signature in the presence of the testator.
- If a beneficiary (the person who gets something under the will) or his or her spouse witnesses the will, then the gift to the beneficiary will not be valid.

Could you apply for reasonable financial provision from the estate?

It should be noted that even if a testator did not make some provision in the will for a particular person, that person may nevertheless be able to apply to the court for some provision. See a solicitor if you think that you may qualify to make such an application, bearing in mind the following basic points:

- you may be a husband or wife, or ex-husband or ex-wife so long as you have not remarried, or a child, including a step-child, or an adopted child, or an illegitimate child
- it should be noted that even someone who is not actually a member of the family, but who, immediately before the testator's death, was being maintained wholly or partly by the testator, may also be eligible to apply
- application must be made to the court within six months of grant of probate or letters of administration.

Power of Attorney

At the time when someone becomes ill, he may execute a Power of Attorney in favour of a relative. If he is not able to manage his affairs, it is the duty of his solicitor, if asked to prepare a Power of Attorney, to be certain that the person fully understands what he is doing.

Enduring Power of Attorney Act 1985

A new act enables the creation of Power of Attorney which will survive any subsequent mental incapacity of the donor to make provision in connection with such powers.

For more details consult a solicitor.

The Court of Protection

The Court is there to look after the property of a person who cannot manage his own affairs because of mental disorder. Under the 1959 Mental Health Act, the Court may look after nearly all areas of a patient's affairs. But the Court can only step in after it has considered the medical evidence of the patient's mental capacity and has decided that on the evidence the patient cannot manage his own affairs. The medical evidence has to be provided by a qualified doctor.

Who can apply?

The close relatives of a patient may apply to the Court for the appointment of a receiver. If the patient's affairs are complex, a professional (such as a solicitor) may apply for appointment. In the event that no one is willing to act, the Official Receiver may be appointed.

To protect the patient, there is a statutory requirement that when someone applies to the Court the patient must get notice of that application. He will be given the name and address of the person who has applied, and the date and time that the application is to be heard, so if need be he can question the claim of his mental incapacity and object to a receiver being appointed.

How to apply

Applications to the Court of Protection may be made by any person, by instructing a solicitor to process the application, or with the help of the Personal Application Branch of the Court. You should apply to: The Chief Clerk, Court of Protection, 25 Store Street, London, WCIE 7BP.

It is a general policy that a receiver has to have special authority from the Court before he can sell a patient's home. A receiver appointed by the Court must give security (by a bond through an insurance company) to cover the amount of cash that may be in the receiver's hands at any one time, and every year has to submit an account of dealings with the patient's property to the Courts.

Unprincipled receivers who refuse to release monies for the patient's general needs – for instance while the patient is in hospital – can be reported by other professionals, who can apply to the Court of Protection for an order requiring the receiver to meet the patient's needs.

If a patient recovers and produces substantiating medical evidence of his recovery, he can apply for the receiver to be discharged.

APPENDIX

Useful Addresses

Abbeyfield Society

186–92 Darkes Lane
Potters Bar
Hertfordshire EN6 1AB　　(Telephone: Potters Bar 44845)

Age Concern

Age Concern England
Bernard Sunley House
60 Pitcairn Road
Mitcham
Surrey CR4 3LL

Age Concern Scotland
33 Castle Street
Edinburgh EH2 3DN

Age Concern Wales
1 Park Grove
Cardiff
CF1 3BJ

Provides advice and information; some day centres.

Alzheimer's Disease Society

40 Shandwick Place
Edinburgh
Scotland　　　　(Telephone: 031-225 1453)

The head office will provide details of your local contact person or
carer's group, and of your nearest regional office.

Anchor

159 Clapham High Street
London sw4   (Telephone: 01-720 7641)

British Red Cross Society

9 Grosvenor Crescent
London swi 7ej   (Telephone: 01-235 5454)

Publishes manuals on caring for the sick.

Chest, Heart and Stroke Association

Tavistock House (North)
Tavistock Square
London wci̅h̅ 9je   (Telephone: 01-387 3012)

Provides useful leaflets for sufferers and their relatives.

Citizens' Advice Bureau

Look in your phone book for the address of the local office. Helps
with information on benefits and services in your area.

Counsel and Care for the Elderly

131 Middlesex Street
London ei 7jf   (Telephone: 01-621 1624)

Keeps a list of inspected homes in the London Area, and gives
advice to relatives. Gives information on private nursing home
charges.

Crossroads Care Attendant Trust

94 Coton Road
Rugby, Warwickshire
CV21 4LN   (Telephone: 0788-73653)

Supplies a care attendant to go into patient's home to supplement existing statutory services in many areas.

Disabled Living Foundation

380–384 Harrow Road
London W9 2HU   (Telephone: 01-289 6111)

Has brochures and aids for the disabled on display.

GRACE

PO Box 71
Cobham
Surrey ST11 2JR   (Telephone: 01-266 5765)

Has details of private homes outside London.

Marie Curie Memorial Foundation

28 Belgrave Square
London SW1X 8QG   (Telephone: 01-235 3325)

Can provide a night nurse for sufferers. Ask your district nurse for details.

Mind

22 Harley Street
London WIN 2ED   (Telephone: 01-637 0741)

Advises the relations of mentally infirm people. Local organizations – look in your phone book for the local branch.

National Council for Carers and their Elderly Dependants (*NCCED*)

29 Chilworth Mews
London W2 3RG   (Telephone: 01-262 1451)

The established caring organization, with expertise on advising carers of the elderly.

National Society for Cancer Relief

Michael Sobell House
30 Dorset Square
London NWI 6OL   (Telephone: 01-402 8125)

Provides financial help to pay final costs or buy extra bedding.

Parkinson's Disease Society

36 Portland Place
London WIN 3DG   (Telephone: 01-323 1174)

Advises sufferers' families on coping with everyday problems.

Royal Institute for the Deaf

105 Gower Street
London WC1E 6AH   (Telephone: 01-387 8033)

Advises on coping with deafness.

Royal National Institute for the Blind

224 Great Portland Street
London W1N 6AA   (Telephone: 01-388 1266)

Gives guidance on coping with blindness.

St John Ambulance Association

1 Grosvenor Crescent
London SW1X 7EF   (Telephone: 01-235 5231)

First aid through classes and pamphlets. Provides services to help the sick and handicapped.

Volunteer Bureau

25 Tavistock Place
London WC1   (Telephone: 01-388 2071)

Women's Royal Voluntary Service

Look in your phone book for the local branch.

Index

Index

Useful Telephone Numbers

General practitioner _____

District nurse _____

Health visitor _____

Social services _____

Ambulance _____

Dentist _____

Eye doctor _____

Neighbour _____

Taxi _____

MORE ABOUT PENGUINS, PELICANS, PEREGRINES AND PUFFINS

For further information about books available from Penguins please write to Dept EP, Penguin Books Ltd, Harmondsworth, Middlesex UB7 0DA.

In the U.S.A.: For a complete list of books available from Penguins in the United States write to Dept DG, Penguin Books, 299 Murray Hill Parkway, East Rutherford, New Jersey 07073.

In Canada: For a complete list of books available from Penguins in Canada write to Penguin Books Canada Ltd, 2801 John Street, Markham, Ontario L3R 1B4.

In Australia: For a complete list of books available from Penguins in Australia write to the Marketing Department, Penguin Books Australia Ltd, P.O. Box 257, Ringwood, Victoria 3134.

In New Zealand: For a complete list of books available from Penguins in New Zealand write to the Marketing Department, Penguin Books (N.Z.) Ltd, Private Bag, Takapuna, Auckland 9.

In India: For a complete list of books available from Penguins in India write to Penguin Overseas Ltd, 706 Eros Apartments, 56 Nehru Place, New Delhi 110019.

A CHOICE OF PENGUINS

☐ *Small World* **David Lodge** £2.50

A jet-propelled academic romance, sequel to *Changing Places.* 'A new comic débâcle on every page' – *The Times.* 'Here is everything one expects from Lodge but three times as entertaining as anything he has written before' – *Sunday Telegraph*

☐ *The Neverending Story* **Michael Ende** £3.95

The international bestseller, now a major film: 'A tale of magical adventure, pursuit and delay, danger, suspense, triumph' – *The Times Literary Supplement*

☐ *The Sword of Honour Trilogy* **Evelyn Waugh** £3.95

Containing *Men at Arms, Officers and Gentlemen* and *Unconditional Surrender*, the trilogy described by Cyril Connolly as 'unquestionably the finest novels to have come out of the war'.

☐ *The Honorary Consul* **Graham Greene** £2.50

In a provincial Argentinian town, a group of revolutionaries kidnap the wrong man . . . 'The tension never relaxes and one reads hungrily from page to page, dreading the moment it will all end' – Auberon Waugh in the *Evening Standard*

☐ *The First Rumpole Omnibus* **John Mortimer** £4.95

Containing *Rumpole of the Bailey, The Trials of Rumpole* and *Rumpole's Return*. 'A fruity, foxy masterpiece, defender of our wilting faith in mankind' – *Sunday Times*

☐ *Scandal* **A. N. Wilson** £2.25

Sexual peccadillos, treason and blackmail are all ingredients on the boil in A. N. Wilson's new, *cordon noir* comedy. 'Drily witty, deliciously nasty' – *Sunday Telegraph* .

A CHOICE OF PENGUINS

☐ *Stanley and the Women* **Kingsley Amis**   £2.50

'Very good, very powerful . . . beautifully written . . . This is Amis *père* at his best' – Anthony Burgess in the *Observer*. 'Everybody should read it' – *Daily Mail*

☐ *The Mysterious Mr Ripley* **Patricia Highsmith**   £4.95

Containing *The Talented Mr Ripley, Ripley Underground* and *Ripley's Game*. 'Patricia Highsmith is the poet of apprehension' – Graham Greene. 'The Ripley books are marvellously, insanely readable' – *The Times*

☐ *Earthly Powers* **Anthony Burgess**   £4.95

'Crowded, crammed, bursting with manic erudition, garlicky puns, omnilingual jokes . . . (a novel) which meshes the real and personalized history of the twentieth century' – Martin Amis

☐ *Life & Times of Michael K* **J. M. Coetzee**   £2.95

The Booker Prize-winning novel: 'It is hard to convey . . . just what Coetzee's special quality is. His writing gives off whiffs of Conrad, of Nabokov, of Golding, of the Paul Theroux of *The Mosquito Coast*. But he is none of these, he is a harsh, compelling new voice' – Victoria Glendinning

☐ *The Stories of William Trevor*   £5.95

'Trevor packs into each separate five or six thousand words more richness, more laughter, more ache, more multifarious human-ness than many good writers manage to get into a whole novel' – *Punch*

☐ *The Book of Laughter and Forgetting*
Milan Kundera   £3.95

'A whirling dance of a book . . . a masterpiece full of angels, terror, ostriches and love . . . No question about it. The most important novel published in Britain this year' – Salman Rushdie

A CHOICE OF
PELICANS AND PEREGRINES

A CHOICE OF
PELICANS AND PEREGRINES

☐ *A Question of Economics* **Peter Donaldson** £4.95

Twenty key issues – from the City and big business to trades unions –
clarified and discussed by Peter Donaldson, author of *10 × Economics* and one of our greatest popularizers of economics.

☐ *Inside the Inner City* **Paul Harrison** £4.95

A report on urban poverty and conflict by the author of *Inside the
Third World*. 'A major piece of evidence' – *Sunday Times*. 'A classic:
it tells us what it is really like to be poor, and why' – *Time Out*

☐ *What Philosophy Is* **Anthony O'Hear** £4.95

What are human beings? How should people act? How do our
thoughts and words relate to reality? Contemporary attitudes to
these age-old questions are discussed in this new study, an eloquent
and brilliant introduction to philosophy today.

☐ *The Arabs* **Peter Mansfield** £4.95

New Edition. 'Should be studied by anyone who wants to know
about the Arab world and how the Arabs have become what they are
today' – *Sunday Times*

☐ *Religion and the Rise of Capitalism*
   R. H. Tawney £3.95

The classic study of religious thought of social and economic issues
from the later middle ages to the early eighteenth century.

☐ *The Mathematical Experience*
   Philip J. Davis and Reuben Hersh £7.95

Not since *Gödel, Escher, Bach* has such an entertaining book been
written on the relationship of mathematics to the arts and sciences.
'It deserves to be read by everyone ... an instant classic' – *New
Scientist*

A CHOICE OF
PELICANS AND PEREGRINES

☐ *Crowds and Power* **Elias Canetti**   £4.95

'Marvellous . . . an immensely interesting, often profound reflection about the nature of society, in particular the nature of violence' – Susan Sontag in *The New York Review of Books*

☐ *The Death and Life of Great American Cities*
Jane Jacobs   £5.95

One of the most exciting and wittily written attacks on contemporary city planning to have appeared in recent years – thought-provoking reading and, as one critic noted, 'extremely apposite to conditions in the UK'.

☐ *Computer Power and Human Reason*
Joseph Weizenbaum   £3.95

Internationally acclaimed by scientists and humanists alike: 'This is the best book I have read on the impact of computers on society, and on technology and on man's image of himself' – *Psychology Today*

These books should be available at all good bookshops or news-agents, but if you live in the UK or the Republic of Ireland and have difficulty in getting to a bookshop, they can be ordered by post. Please indicate the titles required and fill in the form below.

NAME _____ BLOCK CAPITALS

ADDRESS _____

_____

_____

Enclose a cheque or postal order payable to The Penguin Bookshop to cover the total price of books ordered, plus 50p for postage. Readers in the Republic of Ireland should send £IR equivalent to the sterling prices, plus 67p for postage. Send to: The Penguin Book-shop, 54/56 Bridlesmith Gate, Nottingham, NG1 2GP.

You can also order by phoning (0602) 599295, and quoting your Barclaycard or Access number.

Every effort is made to ensure the accuracy of the price and availability of books at the time of going to press, but it is sometimes necessary to increase prices and in these circumstances retail prices may be shown on the covers of books which may differ from the prices shown in this list or elsewhere. This list is not an offer to supply any book.

This order service is only available to residents in the UK and the Republic of Ireland.